Cake
Favourites

Paré • Darcy

Distributed by
Canada Book Distributors
www.canadabookdistributors.com
Tel: 1-800-661-9017

Library and Archives Canada Cataloguing in Publication

Title: Cake favourites / Paré, Darcy.
Names: Paré, Jean, author. | Darcy, James, 1956- author.
Identifiers: Canadiana 20200193465 | ISBN 9781772070651 (softcover)
Subjects: LCSH: Cake. | LCGFT: Cookbooks.
Classification: LCC TX771 .P37 2020 | DDC 641.86/53—dc23

Front Cover: GettyImages: serezniy; panida wijitpanya.
Back Cover, Front Flap & Back Flap: Company's Coming; GettyImages: NoirChocolate; istetiana.

All inside photos by Company's Coming except: from GettyImages: A_Lein, 31, 49; AbbieImages, 85; Anna_Shepulova, 135; AnnapolisStudios, 35; ArxOnt, 7; ASIFE, 45; belchonock, 61; bhofack2, 37; Sonia Bozzo, 55; brebca, 5; Liubov Mernaya Charignon, 89; IngridHS, 75; irene_k, 9; istetiana, 47; Jordanlye, 137; Jupiterimages, 59; KateSmirnova, 21, 157; leelakajonkij, 87; letterberry, 117; manyakotic, 29, 101; October22, 63; Marta Ortiz, 25; NoirChocolate, 91; pamela_d_mcadams, 33; QuietJosephine, 53; Jen Tepp, 119; Tuned_In, 43.

We acknowledge the financial support of the Government of Canada.
Nous reconnaissons l'appui financier du gouvernement du Canada.

Funded by the Government of Canada
Financé par le gouvernement du Canada | Canadä

PC: 38-1

Table of Contents

The Jean Paré Story

Jean Paré (pronounced "jeen PAIR-ee") grew up understanding that the combination of family, friends and home cooking is the best recipe for a good life. When Jean left home, she took with her a love of cooking, many family recipes and an intriguing desire to read cookbooks as if they were novels!

"Never share a recipe you wouldn't use yourself."

When her four children had all reached school age, Jean volunteered to cater the 50th anniversary celebration of the Vermilion School of Agriculture, now Lakeland College, in Alberta, Canada. Working from her home, Jean prepared a dinner for more than 1,000 people and from there launched a flourishing catering operation that continued for more than 18 years.

As requests for her recipes increased, Jean was often asked, "Why don't you write a cookbook?" The release of *150 Delicious Squares* on April 14, 1981, marked the debut of what would soon turn into one of the world's most popular cookbook series.

Company's Coming cookbooks are distributed in Canada, the United States, Australia and other world markets. Bestsellers many times over in English, Company's Coming cookbooks have also been published in French and Spanish.

Familiar and trusted in home kitchens around the world, Company's Coming cookbooks are offered in a variety of formats. Highly regarded as kitchen workbooks, the softcover Original Series, with its lay-flat plastic comb binding, is still a favourite among home cooks.

Jean Paré's approach to cooking has always called for quick and easy recipes using everyday ingredients. That view served her well, and the tradition continues in the Practical Gourmet series.

Jean's Golden Rule of Cooking is: Never share a recipe you wouldn't use yourself. It's an approach that has worked—millions of times over!

Introduction

Who doesn't love cake? Whether it is a simple pound cake or a decadent, drool-worthy chocolate masterpiece, cake is one of those things that brings a smile to your face and a lightness to your heart.

No matter what the celebration, there is sure to be a cake on the table. Birthdays, weddings, graduations, Christmas parties…no event would be complete without a cake to be shared and enjoyed. But you don't need to wait for a special occasion to indulge in a slice. Cakes can make every day worth celebrating. Whether you are having coffee with a friend, gathering with family for the holidays or just unwinding after a long day, a slice of cake makes your day extra special.

The cakes in this book are simple to prepare and for the most part use everyday ingredients you probably have on hand in your kitchen or pantry. We've included everything from classic favourites, such as Devil's Food Cake and Red Velvet Cake, to fun novelty cakes, such as Mocha Cake Pops and Cone Cupcakes. And, of course, no cake book would be complete without a selection of cheesecakes, tortes and chilled or frozen selections. No matter how you slice it, this book has a cake for everyone and every occasion.

Tips for Success

Does this sound familiar? You want to treat your family and friends to a special something sweet, so you pull out your favourite cake ingredients, whip up the batter and toss the pan into the oven. The timer lets you know the cake is done, but instead of pulling out a light, fluffy, mouth-watering cake, you have a dense, chewy disappointment. You ask yourself, What could possibly have gone wrong? Fret not. We have assembled a list of helpful tips to help prevent such a tragedy from occurring in your kitchen.

Preheat your oven. This may not be an important step when cooking a roast or a casserole, but for more delicate baked goods (think cakes, breads, cookies and the like) it is crucial. Baking is basically culinary chemistry. You get the delicious end result thanks to the way the ingredients interact during the baking process. Many ingredients, including baking powder, baking soda, eggs and butter, need specific temperatures to be activated, so they can work their magic. If you put your cake batter into a cold or warming oven, you will get a dense, unappealing cake.

Make sure your ingredients are at room temperature. Using cold ingredients can lead to overmixing because they do not combine as well. Take items such as butter, milk, eggs out of the fridge at least 30 minutes before you plan to start preparing the batter to give them time to warm up naturally. Butter creams better when it is at room temperature and holds more air, which gives your cake a light, fluffy texture. Adding cold liquid or eggs to your creamed butter solidifies the butter, which in turn affects the texture of your cake. Using cold ingredients also reduces the temperature of your batter, which can affect the baking time.

Eggs. Separate eggs when they are cold (a cold egg separates better than a warm one) but then bring them to room temperature before use.

Spoon in dry ingredients. When measuring your ingredients, don't scoop powdery ingredients such as flour, icing sugar or cocoa into the measuring cups. Scooping packs the ingredient too tightly, so you get more than the recipe calls for. Instead, spoon your ingredient into your measuring cup, and don't pat it down or bang the cup against the counter to level it. Run the back of a knife over the top of the measuring cup to level the ingredient in the cup.

Do not overmix the batter. Overmixing will cause your cake will be tough and dense. When flour mixes with liquid, gluten bonds are formed. The more you mix, the stronger the gluten bonds become, and the tougher the end product will be. Overmixing also releases air that has been trapped in the butter during the creaming stage of the recipe. You want as much air trapped in the butter as possible because this is what helps to make your cake light and fluffy.

Bake cakes in the centre of your oven, unless the recipe specifies otherwise. This is where they will bake most evenly.

Check your cake for doneness at least 5 minutes before the recommended cooking time has passed. All ovens are different, and what takes 25 minutes to cook in someone else's oven might take only 20 in yours.

Don't throw out that stale cake! Crumble it up and sprinkle it over ice cream for a delicious topping, or freeze it and make cake pops on another day!

Storage Tips

Refrigerate any cakes that have a whipped cream or cream cheese icing, or that have a fresh fruit filling.

Wrap un-iced cakes tightly with plastic wrap to keep them fresh. You want to keep air away from any of the cake's surfaces to keep it from drying out. A well-wrapped, un-iced cake can be stored at room temperature for about 5 days if uncut, and about 3 to 4 days once it has been cut. For a cut cake, press plastic wrap directly against the sliced edge to keep air away from it, and then wrap the entire cake tightly with plastic wrap. Freeze your cakes if you need to store them longer than 5 days.

Most iced cakes will last for 3 to 4 days on the counter, as long as they are well protected from drying out. You can wrap the cake in plastic wrap, but you run the risk of smooshing your icing. Instead, press a piece of plastic wrap directly against any cut edges so that it sticks in place and forms a barrier against the drying air, and then cover the entire cake with a large bowl. You can also stick several toothpicks into the top and sides of the cake and then cover it with plastic wrap. The toothpicks will keep the wrap from touching the icing.

To freeze your cake, make sure the cake has cooled completely before wrapping it first in plastic wrap and then in a layer of aluminum foil. Put the wrapped cake in a container if you have one that fits as an extra layer of protection in the freezer. Cakes will stay fresh in the freezer for about 3 months. They will still be safe to eat after the 3-month mark, but the quality starts to deteriorate the longer they are frozen.

Do not unwrap frozen cakes to thaw them. Place them in the fridge or on the counter still wrapped snugly in their plastic wrap and aluminum foil barrier. Condensation will form on the wrapping as the cake thaws. You want this moisture to stay on the wrapping and away from the cake, otherwise the cake will become mushy.

Rhubarb Coffee Cake

This tender cake is loaded with tart rhubarb and topped with a crunchy cinnamon topping. What spring treat could be better?

Brown sugar, packed	1/2 cup	125 mL
All-purpose flour	1 tbsp.	15 mL
Ground cinnamon	1 tsp.	5 mL
Butter (or hard margarine)	1 tbsp.	15 mL
Butter (or hard margarine)	1/2 cup	125 mL
Granulated sugar	1 1/2 cups	375 mL
Large eggs	2	2
Sour cream	1 cup	250 mL
Vanilla extract	1 tsp.	5 mL
All-purpose flour	2 cups	500 mL
Baking soda	1 tsp.	5 mL
Finely cut rhubarb	2 cups	500 mL

For the topping, combine first 3 ingredients in a medium bowl. Cut in first amount of butter until mixture resembles coarse crumbs. Set aside.

Cream second amount of butter and sugar together in a large bowl. Add eggs 1 at a time, beating well after each addition.

Stir in sour cream and vanilla.

Combine flour and baking soda in a small bowl. Fold into butter mixture.

Stir in rhubarb. Spread batter evenly in a greased 9 x 13 inch (23 x 33 cm) pan. Sprinkle topping over batter. Bake in 350°F (175°C) oven for 30 to 40 minutes until a wooden pick inserted in centre comes out clean. Cuts into 18 pieces.

Coffee Streusel Cake

Instant coffee granules make this a coffee cake in more ways than one. Not only does this moist treat go well with your favourite cup of java, but it's infused with a lovely coffee flavour.

Brown sugar, packed	3/4 cup	175 mL
All-purpose flour	1/3 cup	75 mL
Chopped walnuts	1/3 cup	75 mL
Medium, unsweetened coconut	1/3 cup	75 mL
Ground cinnamon	1 tsp.	5 mL
Butter (or hard margarine), softened	1/4 cup	60 mL
Butter (or hard margarine), softened	1/2 cup	125 mL
Granulated sugar	3/4 cup	175 mL
Large eggs	2	2
Milk	1/2 cup	125 mL
Instant coffee granules	1 tbsp.	15 mL
Vanilla extract	1 tsp.	5 mL
All-purpose flour	1 1/2 cups	375 mL
Chopped walnuts	2/3 cup	150 mL
Baking powder	1 tbsp.	15 mL
Ground cinnamon	1 tsp.	5 mL
Ground nutmeg	1/2 tsp.	2 mL

For the streusel, combine first 5 ingredients in a medium bowl. Cut in first amount of butter until mixture resembles coarse crumbs. Set aside.

For the cake, beat remaining butter and sugar in a large bowl until light and creamy. Add eggs, 1 at a time, beating well after each addition.

Combine next 3 ingredients in a small bowl. Stir into butter mixture.

Combine remaining 5 ingredients in a separate small bowl. Add to butter mixture and stir well. Spread 1/3 of batter evenly in greased 8 x 8 inch (20 x 20 cm) pan. Sprinkle 1/3 of streusel mixture over batter. Repeat 2 more times with remaining batter and streusel mixture. Bake in 350°F (175°C) oven for about 40 minutes until a wooden pick inserted in centre comes out clean. Cuts into 16 pieces.

Caramel Apple Cake

Caramel, apples and oats—what's not to like? This whole-wheat cake is wholesome and appealing.

Diced peeled cooking apple (such as McIntosh)	2 cups	500 mL
Lemon juice	2 tbsp.	30 mL
Large flake rolled oats	1/2 cup	125 mL
Brown sugar, packed	1/4 cup	60 mL
Butter (or hard margarine), melted	3 tbsp.	45 mL
Ground cinnamon	1 tsp.	5 mL
Whole-wheat flour	1 1/4 cups	300 mL
Baking powder	1 1/2 tsp.	7 mL
Salt	1/2 tsp.	2 mL
Butter (or hard margarine), softened	1/2 cup	125 mL
Granulated sugar	1/2 cup	125 mL
Large egg	1	1
Vanilla extract	1 tsp.	5 mL
Milk	2/3 cup	150 mL
Caramel ice cream topping	1/3 cup	75 mL

Toss apple and lemon juice in a medium bowl.

Stir next 4 ingredients in a small bowl until mixture resembles coarse crumbs. Set aside.

Combine next 3 ingredients in a separate small bowl.

Beat second amount of butter and granulated sugar in a large bowl until light and fluffy.

Add egg and vanilla. Beat well. Add flour mixture in 3 additions, alternating with milk in 2 additions, stirring well after each addition until just combined. Spread in greased 9 x 9 inch (23 x 23 cm) pan. Arrange apple mixture over top.

Drizzle ice cream topping over apple mixture. Sprinkle reserved oat mixture over top. Bake in 350°F (175°C) oven for about 45 minutes until a wooden pick inserted in centre comes out clean. Let stand in pan on wire rack until cool. Cuts into 16 pieces.

Date Cake

It's a good idea to grease your pans and tins, even if they're non-stick. A coating of fat allows the sides of your baking to crisp and makes clean up a snap. We use cooking spray in our test kitchen.

Chopped pitted dates	1 1/2 cups	375 mL
Baking soda	1 1/2 tsp.	7 mL
Boiling water	1 1/2 cups	375 mL
Butter (or hard margarine), softened	3/4 cup	175 mL
Brown sugar, packed	1 cup	250 mL
Granulated sugar	1/2 cup	125 mL
Large eggs	2	2
Vanilla extract	1 tsp.	5 mL
All-purpose flour	2 1/2 cups	625 mL
Baking powder	1 1/2 tsp.	7 mL
Salt	1/2 tsp.	2 mL
Brown sugar, packed	1 cup	250 mL
Butter (or hard margarine)	1/3 cup	75 mL
Half-and-half cream (or milk)	3 tbsp.	45 mL
Fine coconut	1 cup	250 mL

Put dates into a medium bowl and sprinkle with baking soda. Pour boiling water over top. Let stand until cool. Stir.

Beat next 3 ingredients in a large bowl until light and creamy. Add eggs, 1 at a time, beating well after each addition. Beat in vanilla.

Combine next 3 ingredients in a small bowl. Add to butter mixture in 3 additions, alternating with date mixture in 2 additions, beginning and ending with flour mixture. Spread evenly in a greased 9 x 13 inch (23 x 33 cm) pan. Bake in 325°F (160°C) oven for 40 to 50 minutes until a wooden pick inserted in centre comes out clean.

For the topping, combine next 3 ingredients in a medium saucepan. Bring to a rolling boil on medium-high, stirring occasionally. Remove from heat.

Stir in coconut. Spread evenly over warm cake. Bake for about 3 minutes until top is bubbling. Let stand in pan on a wire rack until cool. Cuts into 18 pieces.

Peaches and Cream Cake

Juicy peaches give this cake an almost creamy texture. Serve it with extra peach slices and whipped cream on the side. You can substitute the same size of coconut cream pudding powder (not instant) for the vanilla, if you prefer.

Large egg	1	1
All-purpose flour	1 cup	250 mL
Milk	2/3 cup	150 mL
Box of vanilla pudding powder (not instant), 6-serving size	1	1
Butter (or hard margarine), softened	3 tbsp.	45 mL
Baking powder	1 tsp.	5 mL
Salt	1/2 tsp.	2 mL
Can of sliced peaches in juice (14 oz., 398 mL) drained and juice reserved	1	1
Block of cream cheese (8 oz., 250 g), softened	1	1
Granulated sugar	1/2 cup	125 mL
Reserved peach juice	3 tbsp.	45 mL
Granulated sugar	2 tbsp.	30 mL
Ground cinnamon	1 tbsp.	15 mL

Beat first 7 ingredients in a large bowl until smooth. Spread evenly in a greased 8 x 8 inch (20 x 20 cm) pan.

Arrange peach slices over batter.

Beat next 3 ingredients in a medium bowl until smooth. Drop by tablespoonfuls over peach slices. Spread evenly.

Combine second amount of sugar and cinnamon in a small cup. Sprinkle over cream cheese mixture. Bake in 350°F (175°C) oven for 60 to 70 minutes until a wooden pick inserted in centre comes out clean. Cuts into 16 pieces.

Lemon Coffee Cake

This light coffee cake has a crumb topping and a slightly sweet lemon taste.
Serve it with whipped cream and lemon curd.

All-purpose flour	1/2 cup	125 mL
Brown sugar, packed	1/4 cup	60 mL
Cold butter (or hard margarine), cut up	1/4 cup	60 mL
Finely grated lemon peel	1 tbsp.	15 mL
Milk	1 cup	250 mL
Lemon juice	1 tbsp.	15 mL
Butter (or hard margarine), softened	1/2 cup	125 mL
Granulated sugar	1/2 cup	125 mL
Large eggs	2	2
Finely grated lemon peel	1 tbsp.	15 mL
Vanilla extract	1 tsp.	5 mL
All-purpose flour	2 cups	500 mL
Baking powder	1 1/2 tsp.	7 mL
Baking soda	1/2 tsp.	2 mL
Salt	1/4 tsp.	1 mL

For the topping, combine flour and brown sugar in a medium bowl. Cut in butter until mixture resembles coarse crumbs. Stir in lemon peel. Set aside.

Combine milk and lemon juice in 1 cup (250 mL) liquid measure. Let stand for 10 minutes to sour.

Beat butter and granulated sugar in a large bowl for about 4 minutes until light and creamy. Add eggs, 1 at a time, beating well after each addition. Add lemon peel and vanilla. Stir well.

Combine next 4 ingredients in a small bowl. Add flour mixture to butter mixture in 3 additions, alternating with milk mixture in 2 additions, beginning and ending with flour mixture. Spread in greased 9 x 9 inch (23 x 23 cm) pan. Sprinkle topping evenly over batter. Bake in 350°F (175°C) oven for about 30 to 35 minutes until golden brown and a wooden pick inserted in centre comes out clean. Let stand in pan on a wire rack for 15 minutes. Serve warm. Cuts into 9 pieces.

Blueberry Streusel

This cake is light and buttery, studded with blueberries and topped with a delicious cinnamon streusel. If you decide to serve it with a dollop of ice cream alongside your coffee, we won't judge you.

All-purpose flour	1/3 cup	75 mL
Rolled oats	1/3 cup	75 mL
Brown sugar	1/3 cup	75 mL
Cinnamon	1/2 tsp.	2 mL
Cold butter (or hard margarine), cut up	1/4 cup	60 mL
All-purpose flour	2 cups	500 mL
Baking powder	1 1/4 tsp.	6 mL
Salt	1/2 tsp.	2 mL
Butter (or hard margarine), softened	1/2 cup	125 mL
Granulated sugar	1 cup	250 mL
Large eggs	3	3
Milk	1/2 cup	125 mL
Blueberries (fresh or frozen)	1 cup	250 mL

For the streusel, combine first 4 ingredients in a small bowl. Cut in butter until mixture resembles coarse crumbs. Set aside.

Combine next 3 ingredients in a medium bowl. Set aside.

Cream second amount of butter and sugar in a large bowl. Add eggs 1 at a time, beating well after each addition.

Add flour mixture in 3 parts, alternating with milk in 2 parts, stirring after each addition until just combined. Add blueberries and stir until just combined. Spread in a greased 9 x 5 x 3 inch (23 x 12.5 x 7.5 cm) loaf pan. Sprinkle streusel over batter and pat down gently. Bake in 325°F (160°C) oven for about 1 hour until a wooden pick inserted in centre comes out clean. Let stand in pan on a wire rack for 10 minutes. Cuts into 16 slices.

Cranberry Almond Cake

If you know someone who suffers from a gluten allergy, they're sure to thank you for this delightful festive offering. It is so tasty you would never guess it is gluten free!

Gluten-free all-purpose baking flour (see Note)	2 cups	500 mL
Brown sugar, packed	3/4 cup	175 mL
Ground almonds	3/4 cup	175 mL
Gluten-free baking powder	1 tbsp.	15 mL
Xanthan gum	1 1/2 tsp.	7 mL
Ground cinnamon	1 tsp.	5 mL
Salt	1/2 tsp.	2 mL
Cold butter, cut up	1/2 cup	125 mL
Large eggs, fork-beaten	2	2
Milk	1 1/4 cups	300 mL
Vanilla extract	1 tsp.	5 mL
Chopped frozen cranberries	1 1/2 cups	375 mL
Gluten-free all-purpose baking flour	3/4 cup	175 mL
Brown sugar, packed	1/2 cup	125 mL
Butter, melted	1/3 cup	75 mL
Slivered almonds	1/2 cup	125 mL

Combine first 7 ingredients in a large bowl. Cut in butter until mixture resembles coarse crumbs. Make a well in centre.

Add next 3 ingredients to well and stir until just moistened. Spread evenly in a greased 9 x 9 inch (23 x 23 cm) pan.

Sprinkle cranberries over top.

Combine remaining 4 ingredients in a small bowl until mixture resembles coarse crumbs. Sprinkle evenly over cranberries. Bake in 350°F (175°C) oven for about 1 hour until a wooden pick inserted in centre of cake comes out clean. Let stand in pan on a wire rack for about 15 minutes. Cuts into 9 pieces.

Note: Gluten-free all-purpose baking flour is available at major grocery stores and health food stores. It is different from gluten-free baking mixes, which usually contain leaveners.

Brown Sugar Pound Cake

This is a special cake from the past, before we worried about things like counting calories and fat grams! It is a large nutty, moist cake with an absolutely incredible taste. Dust with icing sugar for a pretty presentation.

All-purpose flour	3 cups	750 mL
Baking powder	1/2 tsp.	2 mL
Salt	1/2 tsp.	2 mL
Butter, softened	1 1/2 cups	375 mL
Brown sugar, packed	4 cups	1 L
Large eggs	5	5
Vanilla extract	1 tsp.	5 mL
Maple extract	1/2 tsp.	2 mL
Milk	1 cup	250 mL
Finely chopped walnuts (or pecans)	1 cup	250 mL

Combine flour, baking powder and salt in a medium bowl.

Cream butter in a large bowl until light and fluffy. Gradually beat in brown sugar. Add eggs, 1 at a time, beating well after each addition. Mix in vanilla and maple extract.

Add flour mixture in 3 parts alternately with milk in 2 parts, beginning and ending with flour mixture. Fold in walnuts. Turn into a greased and floured 10 inch (25 cm) angel food tube pan with a removable bottom. If using a different size pan, fill it only 3/4 full. Bake in 325°F (160°C) oven for 1 1/4 to 1 1/2 hours until a wooden pick inserted in center comes out clean. Let stand in pan for 10 minutes before turning out onto a rack to cool. Cuts into 20 pieces.

Pumpkin Pecan Pound Cake

This moist pumpkin pound cake with crunchy pecans is spectacular topped with a smooth caramel brandy sauce.

Butter (or hard margarine)	1 cup	250 mL
Granulated sugar	2 cups	500 mL
Large eggs	4	4
Can of pure pumpkin (14 oz., 398 mL), (no spices)	1	1
Vanilla extract	2 tsp.	10 mL
All-purpose flour	3 cups	750 mL
Baking powder	2 tsp.	10 mL
Baking soda	1 tsp.	5 mL
Ground cinnamon	1 tsp.	5 mL
Ground allspice	1/2 tsp.	2 mL
Salt	1/4 tsp.	1 mL
Chopped pecans (or walnuts), toasted (see Tip, page 148)	1 cup	250 mL
BRANDY SAUCE		
Brown sugar, packed	1/2 cup	125 mL
Butter	1/3 cup	75 mL
Half-and-half cream	1/2 cup	125 mL
Brandy	2 tbsp.	30 mL

Cream butter and sugar in a large bowl. Add eggs, 1 at a time, beating well after each addition.

Add pumpkin and vanilla in 2 additions, beating well after each addition. Mixture may look slightly curdled.

Combine next 6 ingredients in a medium bowl. Slowly add to pumpkin mixture, beating on low until combined. Fold in pecans. Spread evenly in a greased and floured 12 cup (3 L) Bundt pan. Bake in 350°F (175°C) oven for about 60 minutes until a wooden pick inserted in centre of cake comes out clean. Let stand in pan for 10 minutes. Invert onto a wire rack to cool slightly.

For the sauce, combine brown sugar and second amount of butter in a small saucepan on medium heat. Bring to a boil, stirring constantly. Boil gently, uncovered, for about 5 minutes, without stirring, until slightly thickened. Remove from heat.

Stir in cream and brandy. Drizzle over individual servings. Cake cuts into 12 slices.

Old Time Pound Cake

Pound cakes were so named because the original recipes called for one pound each of butter, flour, eggs and sugar. This large cake has a delicate lemon flavour. If you prefer not to use the lemon glaze, simply dust the cake with icing sugar or serve it with a dollop of whipped cream.

Egg whites (large), room temperature	10	10
Butter (or hard margarine), softened	2 cups	500 mL
Granulated sugar	2 cups	500 mL
Egg yolks (large), fork-beaten	10	10
Baking soda	1/2 tsp.	2 mL
Water	1 tsp.	5 mL
Lemon extract	1 tsp.	5 mL
All-purpose flour	4 cups	1 L
Cream of tartar	1 tsp.	5 mL
LEMON GLAZE		
Icing (confectioner's) sugar	1 cup	250 mL
Lemon juice	1 tbsp.	15 mL

Beat egg whites in a large bowl until stiff. Set aside.

Using same beaters, cream butter and sugar together in a mixing bowl.

Beat in egg yolks. Fold in egg whites.

Dissolve baking soda in water and stir in lemon extract. Fold into butter mixture.

Combine flour and cream of tartar in a large bowl. Sift 1/2 over batter and fold in. Repeat with remaining flour mixture. Spread evenly in a greased and floured 12 cup (3L) Bundt pan. If using a different size pan, fill it only 3/4 full. Bake in 300°F (150°C) oven for about 2 hours until a wooden pick inserted in centre comes out clean.

For the glaze, combine icing sugar and lemon juice in a medium bowl, stirring until smooth. Add more icing sugar if glaze is too thin. Spread over cake. Cuts into 16 pieces.

White Chocolate Pound Cake

White chocolate makes this rich cake decadent and sweet. If you want to cut the sweetness a little, skip the icing and simply dust the cake with icing sugar.

White baking chocolate, cut up	4 oz.	113 g
Skim evaporated milk	1 cup	250 mL
Butter (or hard margarine) softened	1 cup	250 mL
Granulated sugar	1 2/3 cups	400 mL
Large eggs	5	5
All-purpose flour	2 3/4 cups	675 mL
Baking soda	1/2 tsp.	2 mL
Salt	1/2 tsp.	2 mL
WHITE CHOCOLATE GLAZE		
Butter (or hard margarine)	1/2 cup	125 mL
White baking chocolate, cut up	6 oz.	170 g
Icing (confectioner's) sugar	4 cups	1 L
Vanilla extract	1 tsp.	5 mL
Milk	2 tbsp.	30 mL

Combine chocolate and evaporated milk in a medium saucepan on low heat (see Tip, page 140). Cook, stirring often, until smooth. Cool to room temperature.

Cream butter and sugar in a large bowl. Add eggs, 1 at a time, beating well after each addition.

Combine flour, baking soda and salt in a separate bowl. Add to batter in 3 parts, alternately with chocolate mixture in 2 parts, beginning and ending with flour mixture. Pour into a greased and floured 12 cup (3 L) Bundt pan. Bake in 325°F (160°C) oven for about 1 hour until a wooden pick inserted in center comes out clean. Let stand for 20 minutes. Turn out of pan onto a wire rack to cool.

For the icing, melt butter and chocolate in a medium saucepan over hot water, stirring constantly, until smooth (see Tip, page 140). Do not overheat. Remove from heat.

Mix in icing sugar, vanilla and milk, adding more milk or icing sugar as needed for proper consistency. Beat well. Spread over cake allowing glaze to drizzle down sides. Cuts into 16 wedges.

Mock Angel Cake

This cake is a little denser than traditional angel food cake, but it can be used in all the same ways, and it is equally delicious!

All-purpose flour	1 1/2 cups	375 mL
Granulated sugar	1 1/2 cups	375 mL
Baking powder	1 tbsp.	15 mL
Salt	1/4 tsp.	1 mL
Milk	1 1/2 cups	375 mL
Egg whites (large), room temperature	3	3

Combine first 4 ingredients in a sieve or flour sifter. Sift onto a large plate or waxed paper. Sift 3 more times, sifting into a large bowl for 4th sifting.

Heat milk in a small saucepan until just boiling. Remove from heat immediately. Stir into flour mixture until smooth.

Beat egg whites in a medium bowl until stiff. Fold into batter until no streaks remain. Turn into an ungreased 10 inch (25 cm) angel food tube pan with a removable bottom. Bake in 350°F (175°C) oven for about 45 minutes until golden. Invert cake in pan onto a glass bottle for 2 to 3 hours until cooled completely (see Tip, page 44). Turn upright. Run a knife around inside edge of pan to loosen cake. Remove bottom of pan with cake. Run knife around tube and bottom of pan to loosen. Invert cake onto a large serving plate. Cuts into 16 wedges.

Lemon Coconut Angel

No need to prepare the traditional angel food cake for this recipe. It works just as well with a store bought angel food cake, a packaged angel food cake mix or the Mock Angel Cake (see page 32). It is quick to put together, but don't forget to factor in the chilling time. For a nuttier flavour, toast the coconut.

Angel food cake (10 inch, 25 cm, diameter)	1	1
Can of lemon pie filling (19 oz., 540 mL)	1	1
Medium unsweetened coconut	1/2 cup	125 mL
Whipped cream (or frozen whipped topping, thawed)	2 cups	500 mL
Medium unsweetened coconut	1/2 cup	125 mL

Cut cake horizontally into 3 layers. Place largest, bottom layer, cut side up, on a large serving plate.

Transfer 1/2 cup (125 mL) pie filling to a small bowl and set aside. Combine remaining pie filling and first amount of coconut in a separate medium bowl. Spread half of coconut mixture on bottom cake layer. Place centre cake layer over coconut mixture. Spread remaining coconut mixture over centre layer. Cover with smallest, top cake layer, cut side down.

Fold whipped cream into reserved pie filling. Spread over top and sides of cake.

Sprinkle with second amount of coconut. Chill for about 1 hour until filling is firm. Cuts into 16 wedges.

Burnt Sugar Angel Food

The burnt sugar syrup gives this cake a caramel taste that is beyond compare. Add some flair to this dessert by serving it with whipped cream and caramelized sugar. Store remaining syrup in a jar at room temperature for up to 6 months.

Granulated sugar	1 cup	250 mL
Boiling water	1/2 cup	125 mL
Cake flour, sifted	1 cup	250 mL
Icing (confectioner's) sugar	1/2 cup	125 mL
Egg whites (large), room temperature	12	12
Cream of tartar	1 1/2 tsp.	7 mL
Salt	1/4 tsp.	1 mL
Granulated sugar	1 cup	250 mL
Vanilla extract	1 tsp.	5 mL
Maple extract	1/4 tsp.	1 mL

For the burnt sugar syrup, heat first amount of granulated sugar in a large heavy saucepan on medium. Cook, stirring, for about 10 minutes until sugar is dissolved. Brush sides of saucepan with a wet pastry brush to dissolve any sugar crystals. Simmer for about 2 minutes, without stirring, until mixture becomes a dark butterscotch colour. Remove from heat. Slowly and carefully add boiling water. Sugar mixture will sputter furiously. Return to heat and cook, stirring, for about 2 minutes until smooth. Colour should be deep golden brown. Let stand for about 1 hour until cooled completely.

For the cake, sift flour and icing sugar together in a sieve or flour sifter 3 times onto sheets of waxed paper or separate bowls. Set aside.

Beat next 3 ingredients in a large bowl until soft peaks form. Add granulated sugar, 1/4 cup (60 mL) at a time, beating constantly until stiff peaks form and sugar is dissolved.

Add vanilla, maple extract and 3 tbsp. (45 mL) burnt sugar syrup.

Beat until just combined. Sift flour mixture over egg white mixture in 4 parts, folding after each addition until just blended. Spread in ungreased 10 inch (25 cm) angel food tube pan with a removable bottom. Cut through batter gently with knife to remove air pockets. Bake in 375°F (190°C) oven for 35 to 40 minutes until a wooden pick inserted in centre of cake comes out clean. Invert cake in pan onto a glass bottle for about 1 hour until cooled completely (see Tip, page 44). Turn upright. Run a knife around inside edge of pan to loosen cake. Remove bottom of pan with cake. Run knife around tube and bottom of pan to loosen cake. Invert onto a large serving plate. Cuts into 16 wedges.

Orange Chiffon Cake

This light-as-air cake with a lovely orange flavour will turn any evening into a special occasion, especially when served with some fresh fruit and a dollop of whipped cream. Use eggs brought to room temperature for best results.

Cake flour, sifted	2 1/4 cups	550 mL
Granulated sugar	1 1/2 cups	375 mL
Baking powder	1 tbsp.	15 mL
Salt	1 tsp.	5 mL
Egg whites (large), room temperature	1 cup	250 mL
Cream of tartar	1/2 tsp.	2 mL
Egg yolks (large)	5	5
Orange juice	3/4 cup	175 mL
Cooking oil	1/2 cup	125 mL
Grated orange zest (see Tip, page 116)	1 tbsp.	15 mL
Vanilla extract	1 tsp.	5 mL

Measure first 4 ingredients into a sieve or flour sifter over a large bowl. Sift into bowl. Make a well in centre. Set aside.

Beat egg whites and cream of tartar in a separate large bowl until stiff peaks form.

Add remaining 5 ingredients to well in flour mixture. Beat until smooth. Fold about 1/4 of egg white mixture into orange mixture. Add remaining egg white mixture in 2 additions, gently folding after each addition until no white streaks remain. Spread in an ungreased 10 inch (25 cm) angel food tube pan with a removable bottom. Bake in 325°F (160°C) oven for 60 to 70 minutes until a wooden pick inserted in centre of cake comes out clean. Invert cake in pan onto a glass bottle for 2 to 3 hours until cooled completely (see Tip, page 44). Turn upright. Run a knife around inside edge of pan to loosen cake. Remove bottom of pan with cake. Run knife around tube and bottom of pan to loosen. Invert cake onto a large serving plate. Cuts into 20 wedges.

Cream of tartar is tartaric acid, which is a byproduct of the wine industry and is derived from crystals that form inside wine barrels. It is used to stabilize egg whites, to add creaminess to candy and frostings and as a leavener when combined with baking soda.

Amaretto Cherry Chiffon

This tall, pink cake is filled with bits of cherry and toasted almonds in a light chiffon texture. Delightful. Serve with whipped cream and cherries.

All-purpose flour	2 cups	500 mL
Granulated sugar	1 1/4 cups	300 mL
Baking powder	1 tbsp.	15 mL
Salt	1 tsp.	5 mL
Cooking oil	1/2 cup	125 mL
Almond-flavoured liqueur (such as Amaretto)	1/2 cup	125 mL
Maraschino cherry syrup	1/4 cup	60 mL
Egg yolks (large)	6	6
Finely chopped maraschino cherries, drained	1/2 cup	125 mL
Finely chopped sliced almonds, toasted (see Tip, page 148)	1/3 cup	75 mL
Egg whites (large), room temperature	8	8
Cream of tartar	1/2 tsp.	2 mL
Granulated sugar	1/4 cup	60 mL
Icing (confectioner's) sugar, for dusting	1 tbsp.	15 mL

Measure first 4 ingredients into a sieve or flour sifter over a large bowl. Sift into bowl. Make a well in centre.

Add next 4 ingredients to well. Beat on medium for about 1 minute until smooth.

Stir in cherries and almonds.

Beat egg whites and cream of tartar in a separate large bowl with clean beaters until soft peaks form.

Add second amount of sugar, 1 tbsp. (15 mL) at a time while beating, until stiff peaks form and sugar is dissolved. Fold about 1/4 of egg white mixture into egg yolk mixture to lighten. Add egg yolk mixture to remaining egg white mixture in 2 batches, gently folding after each addition until no white streaks remain. Pour into an ungreased 10 inch (25 cm) angel food tube pan with a removable bottom. Spread evenly. Cut through batter with a knife to remove large air spaces. Do not tap pan or press down batter. Bake on bottom rack in 325°F (160°C) oven for 60 to 65 minutes until cake springs back when lightly pressed and a wooden pick inserted in centre of cake comes out clean. Invert cake in pan onto neck of a glass bottle to cool completely (see Tip, page 44). Turn upright. Run a knife around inside edge of pan to loosen cake. Remove bottom of pan with cake. Run knife around bottom and centre tube of pan to loosen cake. Invert onto a serving plate.

Dust with icing sugar. Cuts into 20 wedges.

Poppy Seed Chiffon

This lovely, large cake is dusted with icing sugar, but it would also be amazing drizzled with Warm Caramel Sauce (see page 80) or spread with a lemon or caramel icing.

Milk	3/4 cup	175 mL
Poppy seeds	1/2 cup	125 mL
Cake flour	2 cups	500 mL
Granulated sugar	1 1/2 cups	375 mL
Baking powder	1 tbsp.	15 mL
Salt	1 tsp.	5 mL
Cooking oil	1/2 cup	125 mL
Egg yolks (large), room temperature	7	7
Vanilla extract	2 tsp.	10 mL
Lemon extract	1 tsp.	5 mL
Egg whites (large), room temperature	7	7
Cream of tartar	1/2 tsp.	2 mL
Icing (confectioner's) sugar, for dusting		

Combine milk and poppy seeds in a small bowl. Let stand for 2 hours.

Sift flour, sugar, baking powder and salt into a medium mixing bowl. Make a well in centre.

Add next 4 ingredients to well in order given. Add poppy seed mixture to well. Set aside. Do not beat yet.

In a large mixing bowl, beat egg whites and cream of tartar until very stiff. Using same beaters, beat egg yolk mixture until smooth and light. Pour 1/4 at a time over beaten egg whites, folding in with a rubber spatula until all traces of flour disappear. Do not stir. Pour into an ungreased 10 inch (25 cm) angel food pan with a removable bottom. Bake in 325°F (160°C) oven for 55 minutes. Increase heat to 350°F (175°C) and bake 10 to 15 minutes more until a wooden pick inserted in centre comes out clean. Invert cake in pan onto neck of a glass bottle to cool completely (see Tip, page 44). Turn upright. Run a knife around inside edge of pan to loosen cake. Remove bottom of pan with cake. Run knife around bottom and centre tube of pan to loosen cake. Invert onto a serving plate.

Dust with icing sugar. Cuts into 20 wedges.

True Sponge Cake

This light, airy cake contains no leavening agents. It gets its lovely texture from the beaten eggs.

Egg whites (large), room temperature	6	6
Salt	1/8 tsp.	0.5 mL
Granulated sugar	1 cup	250 mL
Egg yolk (large), room temperature	6	6
Lemon juice	1 tbsp.	15 mL
Grated lemon rind	1 tsp.	5 mL
Cake flour	1 cup	250 mL

Icing (confection's) sugar, for dusting

Beat egg whites and salt in a mixing bowl until soft peaks form.

Sprinkle with about 2 tbsp. (30 mL) sugar at a time, beating constantly, until sugar is dissolved and stiff peaks form. Set aside.

In a small mixing bowl, beat egg yolks, lemon juice and lemon rind until very thick. A thick ribbon should fall from beaters when raised. Transfer to a large bowl. Carefully and gently fold in egg whites.

Sift cake flour in a sieve or flour sifter 3 times. Sift 1/4 flour at a time over batter. Gently fold in until no trace of white remains. Immediately turn into an ungreased 10 inch (25 cm) angel food tube pan with a removable bottom. Bake in 325°F (160°F) oven for 55 to 60 minutes until a wooden pick inserted in centre comes out clean. Invert cake in pan onto neck of a glass bottle to cool completely (see Tip, below). Turn upright. Run a knife around inside edge of pan to loosen cake. Remove bottom of pan with cake. Run knife around bottom and centre tube of pan to loosen cake. Invert onto a serving plate.

Dust with icing sugar. Cuts into 20 wedges.

Tip: Inverting your cake onto a glass bottle ensures the cake doesn't touch the counter as it is cooling. Using a bottle is only necessary if your pan does not have "feet" that keep the cake surface elevated as it cools.

Strawberry Shortcake

Loaded with fresh strawberries and whipped cream, this cake is best when fresh strawberries are in season, but it is a welcome treat any time of the year. To make this dessert even lighter, we've replaced the traditional shortcake with an airier sponge cake.

Large eggs	2	2
Granulated sugar	1/2 cup	125 mL
Vanilla extract	1 tsp.	5 mL
All-purpose flour	1 cup	250 mL
Baking powder	1 tsp.	5 mL
Salt	1/2 tsp.	2 mL
Milk	1/2 cup	125 mL
Butter (or hard margarine)	1 tbsp.	15 mL
Whipping cream	1 cup	250 mL
Granulated sugar	1 tbsp.	15 mL
Vanilla extract	1 tsp.	5 mL
Fresh strawberries, sliced	4 cup	1 L
Berry sugar, for sprinkling		

Beat eggs in a large mixing bowl until frothy. Gradually add first amount of sugar, beating constantly, until mixture is thick. Stir in first amount of vanilla.

Combine flour, baking powder and salt in a medium bowl. Stir into egg mixture.

Heat milk and butter in a small saucepan on medium, stirring often, until combined. Stir into batter. Spread evenly in a greased 9 inch (23 cm) round pan. Bake in 350°F (175°C) oven for 25 to 30 minutes until a wooden pick inserted in centre comes out clean. Let stand in pan on a wire rack for 20 minutes. Remove cake from pan and place on a wire rack to cool completely. Slice cooled cake in half horizontally.

Whip cream, remaining sugar and vanilla together in a mixing bowl until stiff. Spread 1/2 whipped cream over bottom cake layer.

Arrange 1/2 strawberries over whipped cream. Top with remaining cake layer and spread remaining whipped cream over top. Arrange remaining strawberries over whipped cream and sprinkle with berry sugar. Cuts into 12 wedges.

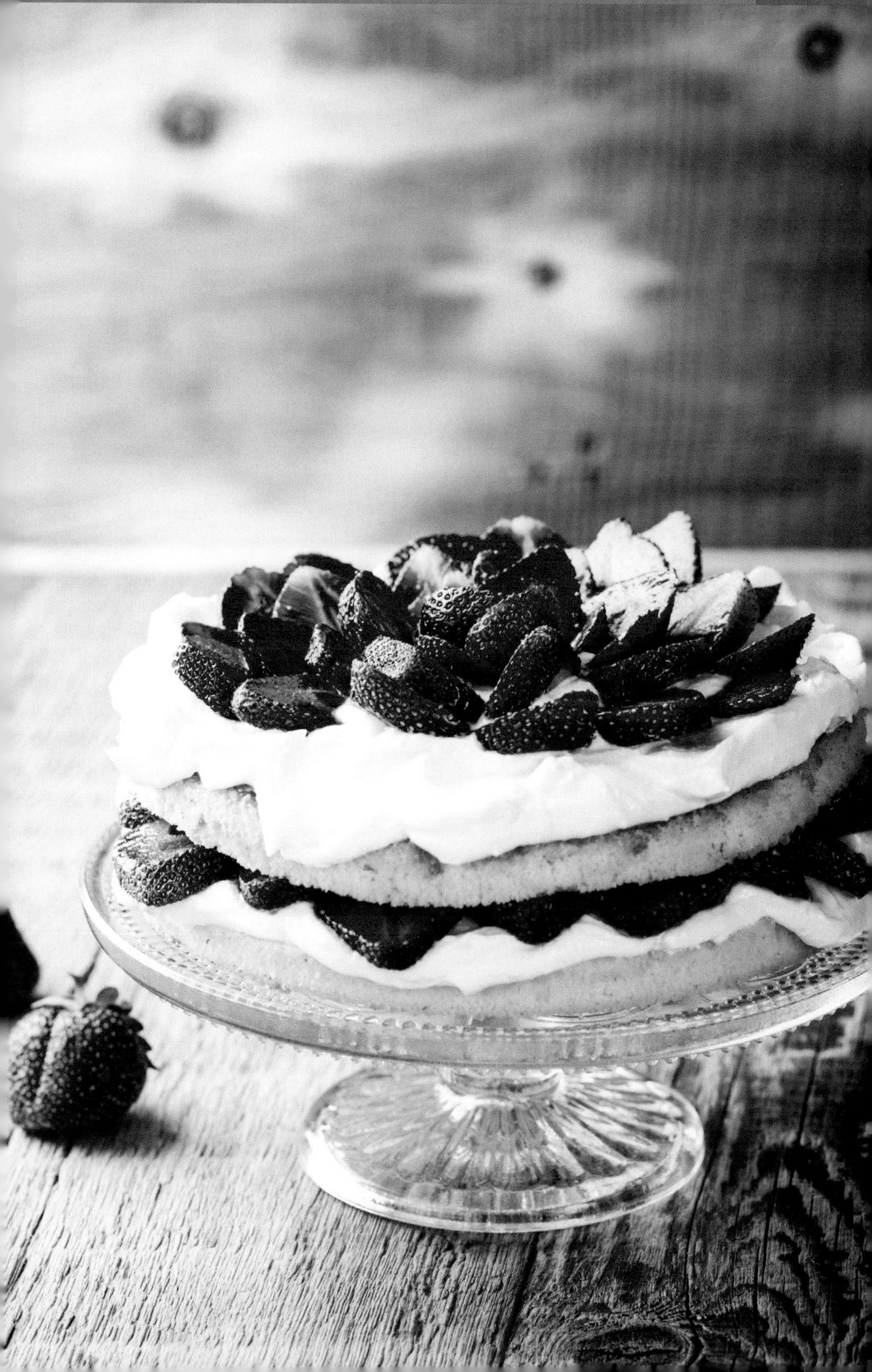

Marbled Sponge Cake

This is a truly beautiful cake, simple to make but elegant enough for any table. It is also delicious without the vanilla and chocolate glazes, but they transform this tasty cake into a visual masterpiece.

Egg whites (large), room temperature	10	10
Cream of tartar	1 tsp.	5 mL
Salt	1/2 tsp.	2 mL
Granulated sugar	1 1/4 cups	300 mL
Cake flour	3/4 cup	175 mL
Egg yolks (large), fork-beaten	6	6
Semi-sweet baking chocolate, melted and cooled (see Tip, page 140)	2 oz.	57 g
Cake flour	1/2 cup	125 mL
Vanilla extract	1 tsp.	5 mL
COCOA GLAZE		
Cocoa, sifted if lumpy	1/4 cup	60 mL
Corn syrup	2 tbsp.	30 mL
Butter (or hard margarine)	2 tbsp.	30 mL
Milk	1/4 cup	60 mL
Vanilla extract	1/4 tsp.	1 mL
Icing (confectioner's) sugar	2 cups	500 mL
VANILLA GLAZE		
Icing (confectioner's sugar)	1 cup	250 mL
Water	1 tbsp.	15 mL
Vanilla extract	1/4 tsp.	1 mL

Beat egg whites in a large bowl until frothy. Add cream of tartar and salt and beat until stiff.

Fold in sugar. Divide batter in half.

Fold first amount of flour, egg yolks and melted chocolate into half of batter.

Fold second amount of flour and vanilla into remaining half of batter. Spoon about 1 cup (250 mL) batter at a time, alternating between colours, into an ungreased 10 inch (25 cm) angel food tube pan with a removable bottom. Bake in 350°F (175°C) oven for about 30 minutes. Reduce heat to 325°F (160°C) and cook for about 20 minutes, until a wooden pik inserted in centre comes out clean. Invert pan onto a rack to cool. Remove cake from pan when completely cooled.

For the cocoa glaze, combine next 5 ingredients in a medium saucepan on low until butter is melted. Remove from heat. Beat in icing sugar, adding more milk or icing sugar as needed to make a barely pourable consistency. Spread over top of cake, allowing glaze to flow down sides. Set aside to cool.

For the vanilla glaze, stir remaining 3 ingredients in a medium bowl until smooth. Drizzle over cocoa glaze, allowing glaze to flow down sides of cake. Cuts into 16 pieces.

Chocolate Mocha Cake

This beautiful, decadent cake is a chocolate masterpiece. Rich without being heavy, it is the perfect indulgent dessert for any occasion!

All-purpose flour	1 3/4 cups	425 mL
Granulated sugar	1 cup	250 mL
Baking soda	1 tsp.	5 mL
Salt	1/2 tsp.	2 mL
Hot strong prepared coffee	1 cup	250 mL
Cocoa, sifted if lumpy	1/2 cup	125 mL
Buttermilk (or soured milk), (see Tip, page 68)	1/2 cup	125 mL
Egg whites (large)	2	2
Vanilla extract	1 tsp.	5 mL
MOCHA FROSTING		
Cold strong prepared coffee	1 cup	250 mL
Box of instant chocolate pudding powder (4 serving size)	1	1
Whipped topping	3 cups	750 mL

Combine first 4 ingredients in a large bowl.

Whisk first amount of coffee and cocoa in a small bowl until cocoa is dissolved.

Combine next 3 ingredients in a medium bowl. Stir in coffee mixture. Add to flour mixture and stir until just combined. Spread evenly in 2 greased 8 inch (20 cm) round pans. Bake in 350°F (175°C) oven for about 20 minutes until a wooden pick inserted in centre comes out clean. Let stand in pans for 10 minutes before inverting onto wire racks to cool completely. Cut each cake in half horizontally to make 4 layers.

For the frosting, beat second amount of coffee and pudding powder in a medium bowl for 2 minutes. Add 1 cup (250 mL) whipped topping and stir until combined. Fold in remaining whipped topping. Chill for 30 minutes. Place 1 cake layer on a serving plate and spread with about 1/2 cup (125 L) frosting. Repeat with second and third cake layers, spreading about 1/2 cup (125 mL) frosting between each layer. Cover with remaining cake layer. Spread remaining frosting over top and sides of cake. Chill for at least 1 hour. Cuts into 8 wedges.

Mississippi Mud Cake

This is a great cake for the whole family! Kids and adults alike will love the fudgy, brownie-like cake topped with gooey marshmallow under a rich chocolate icing. Delicious!

Butter (or hard margarine)	1 cup	250 mL
Cocoa, sifted if lumpy	1/2 cup	125 mL
Granulated sugar	2 cups	500 mL
Large eggs	4	4
All-purpose flour	1 1/2 cups	375 mL
Baking powder	1 tsp.	5 mL
Salt	1/2 tsp.	2 mL
Chopped pecans (or walnuts)	1 1/2 cups	375 mL
Vanilla extract	1 tsp.	5 mL
Jar of marshmallow cream (7 oz., 200 g), or use large marshmallows, cut in half, to cover	1	1

CHOCOLATE ICING

Butter (or hard margarine),	1/4 cup	60 mL
Cocoa, sifted if lumpy	1/3 cup	75 mL
Milk	1/2 cup	125 mL
Icing (confectioner's) sugar	3 cups	750 mL
Vanilla extract	1 tsp.	5 mL

Heat butter and cocoa in a large saucepan over low heat, stirring often, until combined. Remove from heat.

Beat in sugar. Add eggs, 1 at a time, beating well after each addition.

Stir in flour, baking powder and salt.

Stir in pecans and vanilla. Spread in a greased 9 x 13 inch (23 x 33 cm) pan. Bake in 350°F (175°C) oven for 35 to 45 minutes until a wooden pick inserted in centre comes out clean.

For the topping, spread marshmallow cream over hot cake. If you are using marshmallows, cut large ones in half and place cut side down and close together. To hasten melting, place in oven for about 30 seconds, watching carefully to ensure it does not burn.

For the icing, beat remaining 5 ingredients in a large bowl. Spoon over marshmallow topping while still hot and spread gently to give cake a muddied appearance. Cuts into 18 pieces.

Jiffy Chocolate Cake

This is the perfect one-bowl chocolate cake. Quick and simple, but oh so tasty! This cake is delicious as-is, but true chocolate lovers might want to leave off the icing sugar and slather the cake with a creamy Chocolate Ganache (see page 118) instead.

All-purpose flour	1 1/4 cups	300 mL
Granulated sugar	1 cup	250 mL
Cocoa	1/4 cup	60 mL
Butter (or hard margarine), softened	1/4 cup	60 mL
Baking powder	1 tsp.	5 mL
Baking soda	1 tsp.	5 mL
Salt	1/2 tsp.	2 mL
Large egg	1	1
Vanilla extract	1 tsp.	5 mL
Hot water	1 cup	250 mL

Icing (confectioner's) sugar, for dusting

Combine all ingredients in a large mixing bowl in order given and beat until smooth. Spread evenly in a greased 8 inch (20 cm) square pan. Bake in 350°F (175°C) oven for 30 to 40 minutes until a wooden pick inserted in centre comes out clean. Let stand in pan on a wire rack for 20 minutes. Remove cake from pan and place on wire rack.

Dust with icing sugar. Cuts into 12 wedges.

Zucchini Mole Cake

Mole (MOH-lay) is a Mexican sauce made with chocolate and chili spices. We've added the same flair to a moist, decadent chocolate cake with the surprising bite of cayenne. Leftover cake should be stored in the fridge because the icing contains sour cream.

Large eggs	2	2
Granulated sugar	1 3/4 cups	425 mL
Cooking oil	3/4 cup	175 mL
Buttermilk (or soured milk, see Tip, page 68)	1/2 cup	125 mL
Vanilla extract	1 tsp.	5 mL
Almond extract	1/2 tsp.	2 mL
Grated zucchini (with peel)	2 cups	500 mL
All-purpose flour	2 1/2 cups	625 mL
Cocoa, sifted if lumpy	1/3 cup	75 mL
Baking soda	1 tsp.	5 mL
Ground cinnamon	1 tsp.	5 mL
Baking powder	1/2 tsp.	2 mL
Salt	1/2 tsp.	2 mL
Cayenne pepper	1/4 tsp.	1 mL
CHOCOLATE MOLE ICING		
Semi-sweet chocolate chips	1 cup	250 mL
Sour cream	1/2 cup	125 mL
Ground cinnamon	1/2 tsp.	2 mL
Cayenne pepper	1/8 tsp.	0.5 mL

Beat first 6 ingredients in a large bowl until smooth. Stir in zucchini.

Combine next 7 ingredients in a medium bowl. Add to egg mixture and stir until well combined. Spread in a greased 9 x 13 inch (23 x 33 cm) pan. Bake in 350°F (175°C) oven for about 35 minutes until a wooden pick inserted in centre comes out clean. Let stand in pan on a wire rack for 30 minutes. Remove cake from pan and place on wire rack.

For the icing, place chocolate chips and sour cream in a small microwave-safe bowl. Microwave on medium (50%) for about 90 seconds, stirring every 30 seconds until almost melted (see Tip, page 140). Stir until smooth.

Stir in cinnamon and cayenne. Spread over cake and set aside to cool. Cuts into 20 pieces.

Devil's Food Cake

You will not be able to resist this moist, rich, chocolatey cake. It is sinfully delicious!

Cake flour	2 cups	500 mL
Baking soda	1 tsp.	5 mL
Salt	1/4 tsp.	1 mL
Butter (or hard margarine), softened	1/2 cup	125 mL
Brown sugar, packed	1 1/4 cups	300 mL
Large eggs	2	2
Unsweetened baking chocolate, melted (see Tip, page 140)	3 oz.	85 g
Vanilla extract	1 tsp.	5 mL
Milk	1 cup	250 mL

Chocolate Icing, page 52

Sift flour, baking soda and salt together 3 times. Set aside.

In a large mixing bowl, cream butter until light and fluffy. Add sugar and beat well. Add eggs, 1 at a time, beating well after each addition. Add melted chocolate and vanilla. Beat until smooth.

Add milk to butter mixture in 2 parts, alternating with flour mixture in 3 parts, beginning and ending with flour. Divide batter between 2 greased 8 inch (20 cm) round pans. Bake in 350°F (175°C) for about 25 to 30 minutes until a wooden pick inserted in centre comes out clean. Let stand in pan on wire racks for 30 minutes. Remove cakes from pans and place on wire racks to cool completely.

Place 1 cake, top side up, on a plate. Spread with icing. Set second cake over icing, top side up. Spread icing over top and sides of cake. Cuts into 12 wedges.

Chocolate Hazelnut Cake

The rich mocha filling really complements the hazelnut flavour in this gorgeous cake. It is an awesome flavour combination! Garnish with chocolate curls for a lovely presentation.

Large eggs	6	6
Hazelnuts (filberts)	1 1/2 cups	375 mL
Granulated sugar	1 cup	250 mL
Semisweet chocolate chips	1/2 cup	125 mL
Baking powder	4 tsp.	20 mL
Vanilla extract	1 tsp.	5 mL
Salt	1/4 tsp.	1 mL
MOCHA ICING		
Butter or (hard margarine), softened	6 tbsp.	90 mL
Icing (confectioner's) sugar	3 cups	750 mL
Cocoa, sifted if lumpy	3 tsp.	15 mL
Vanilla extract	1 1/2 tsp.	7 mL
Strong coffee	6 tbsp.	90 mL

For the cake, place first 7 ingredients in a blender. Process for 3 minutes. Pour into 2 greased and wax or parchment paper-lined 8 inch (20 cm) round cake layer pans. Bake in 350°F (175°C) oven for about 25 minutes until a wooden pick inserted in center comes out clean. Set aside to cool.

For the icing, beat butter, icing sugar, cocoa, vanilla and coffee together well in a small bowl. Place 1 cake, top side up, on a plate. Spread with icing. Set second cake over icing, top side up. Spread icing over top and sides of cake. Cuts into 12 wedges.

Chocolate Fudge Cake

Chocolate lovers will love this gorgeous cake! Three layers of chocolate fudge cake with a rich fudgy icing. Chocolaty heaven!

Cake flour	2 1/2 cups	550 mL
Baking soda	2 tsp.	10 mL
Salt	1/2 tsp.	2 mL
Butter (or hard margarine), softened	1/2 cup	125 mL
Brown sugar, packed	2 1/2 cups	625 mL
Large eggs	3	3
Vanilla extract	1 1/2 tsp.	7 mL
Unsweetened baking chocolate, melted (see Tip, page 140)	3 oz.	85 g
Sour cream	1 cup	250 mL
Boiling water	1 cup	250 mL
BOILED CHOCOLATE ICING		
Brown sugar, packed	1 cup	250 mL
Water	1/2 cup	125 mL
Butter (or hard margarine)	6 tbsp.	90 mL
Cocoa	1/4 cup	60 mL
Icing (confectioner's) sugar	2 cups	500 mL
Vanilla extract	2 tsp.	10 mL

Combine flour, baking soda and salt in a medium bowl. Set aside.

Cream first amount of butter and brown sugar in a mixing bowl until light and fluffy. Add eggs 1 at a time, beating well between additions. Stir in vanilla and melted chocolate.

Add sour cream to butter mixture in 2 parts and flour mixture in 3 parts, beginning and ending with flour.

Stir in boiling water. Spread evenly in 3 greased 9 inch (23 cm) round pans. Bake in 350°F (175°C) oven for about 35 minutes until a wooden pick inserted in centre comes out clean. Let stand in pans on a wire rack for 10 minutes. Remove to wire racks to cool completely.

For the icing, combine next 4 ingredients in a medium saucepan on medium heat. Bring to a boil and cook for 3 minutes. Remove from heat and set aside to cool.

Stir in icing sugar and vanilla, adding more icing sugar if necessary for your preferred consistency. Set first cake on a plate, top side up, and spread with icing. Repeat with second and third layers. Cover top and sides of cake with icing. Cuts into 12 wedges.

Jelly Roll Cake

Wow your guests with this unique cake. You will no doubt be asked how you did this. Each slice has several rows of cake in it.

Large eggs, room temperature	8	8
Granulated sugar	1 1/2 cups	375 mL
Water	1/4 cup	60 mL
Vanilla extract	2 tsp.	10 mL
Cake flour, sifted	1 1/2 cups	375 mL
Baking powder	2 tsp.	10 mL
Salt	1/2 tsp.	2 mL
Icing (confectioner's) sugar, for dusting		

CHOCOLATE CARAMEL FILLING

Envelopes of dessert topping (not prepared)	2	2
Milk	1 cup	250 mL
Cocoa, sifted if lumpy	1/4 cup	60 mL
Icing (confectioner's) sugar	1/4 cup	60 mL
Salt	1/8 tsp.	0.5 mL
Chocolate toffee candy bar	3	3
(such as Skor), 1 1/2 oz., 39 g each, finely chopped		

Beat eggs in a large bowl until smooth. Add sugar. Beat until light-colored and thick.

Stir in water and vanilla.

Using a sieve or flour sifter, sift flour, baking powder and salt over batter. Fold in. Grease two 10 x 15 inch (25 x 38 cm) jelly roll pans. Line with greased waxed paper. Divide batter evenly between prepared pans. Bake, 1 pan at a time, in 400°F (200°C) oven for 12 to 15 minutes until a wooden pick inserted in center comes out clean. Cool cakes enough to handle. Sift icing sugar onto 2 tea towels. Turn out cakes onto towels. Roll cakes up from narrow end, with towels. Set aside to cool.

For the filling, beat dessert topping and milk in a medium bowl until stiff.

Add cocoa and beat well. Beat in icing sugar and salt. Fold in chopped candy bar. To assemble cake, unroll jelly rolls. Using a ruler, cut each into 3 lengthwise portions of equal width. Spread each cake strip with 1/3 cup (75 mL) filling. Carefully roll up 1 strip like a jelly roll. Set roll on cut edge on a plate. Wind second strip around roll, beginning where first strip ended. Repeat with 4 remaining strips. Ice top and sides of cake with remaining icing. Chill. Cuts into 16 wedges.

Cherry Upside-down Cake

The classic upside-down cake is made with pineapple, but the traditional fruit glaze topping shines best when paired with sweet cherries.

Butter (or hard margarine), softened	3 tbsp.	45 mL
Brown sugar	6 tbsp.	90 mL
Fresh sweet cherries, pitted and halved	1 lb.	454 g
All-purpose flour	1 cup	250 mL
Granulated sugar	2/3 cup	150 mL
Baking powder	2 tsp.	10 mL
Salt	1/2 tsp.	2 mL
Ground nutmeg	1/8 tsp.	0.5 mL
Milk	1/2 cup	125 mL
Butter (or hard margarine), softened	1/3 cup	75 mL
Vanilla extract	1 tsp.	5 mL
Large egg	1	1
Whipping cream	1/2 cup	125 mL
Granulated sugar	1 tsp.	5 mL

Preheat oven to 350°F (175°C). Melt first amount of butter in a greased 8 inch (20 cm) round baking pan in preheating oven. Stir in brown sugar and spread evenly over bottom of pan. Starting at outer edge, arrange cherries, cut side up, in a single layer on bottom of pan, pressing down lightly to make them stick. Set aside.

In a large bowl, combine flour, first amount of granulated sugar, baking powder, salt and nutmeg.

Stir in milk, second amount of butter and vanilla. Beat in egg. Spread batter carefully over cherries. Bake for 35 to 40 minutes, until a wooden pick inserted in centre comes out clean. Let cool in pan on a wire rack for 5 minutes. Loosen edges with a knife, then invert cake onto a platter and let stand for 1 minute or so before removing pan. Allow to cool for about 45 minutes.

Whip cream and second amount of granulated sugar together until stiff. Add a spoonful of whipped cream to each serving. Cuts into 8 wedges.

Citrus Polenta Cake

To further add to the sophistication, brush this lovely cake with orange-flavoured liqueur while it's still warm, add a sprinkle of icing sugar, or garnish with orange wedges. This can also be made into a gluten-free recipe by using gluten-free baking powder.

Ground almonds	1 1/2 cups	375 mL
Yellow cornmeal	1 cup	250 mL
Baking powder	2 tsp.	10 mL
Baking soda	1/2 tsp.	2 mL
Salt	1/4 tsp.	1 mL
Large eggs	2	2
Buttermilk (or soured milk, see Tip, below)	1 1/4 cups	300 mL
Granulated sugar	2/3 cup	150 mL
Olive (or cooking) oil	1/3 cup	75 mL
Lemon juice	2 tbsp.	30 mL
Orange juice	2 tbsp.	30 mL
Grated lemon zest (see Tip, page 116)	1 tsp.	5 mL
Grated orange zest (see Tip, page 116)	1 tsp.	5 mL

Combine first 5 ingredients in a large bowl.

Beat remaining 8 ingredients in a medium bowl. Add to cornmeal mixture and beat well. Pour into a greased 9 inch (23 cm) springform pan. Bake in 350°F (175°C) oven for about 35 minutes until a wooden pick inserted in centre of cake comes out clean. Let stand on a wire rack until cool. Cuts into 12 wedges.

Tip: If a recipe calls for soured milk, measure 1 tbsp. (15 mL) white vinegar or lemon juice into a 1 cup (250 mL) liquid measure. Add enough milk to make 1 cup (250 mL). Stir and let stand for 1 minute.

Gingerbread Bundt

This beautifully dark Bundt cake is perfect for festive get-togethers. Cocoa, applesauce and beer contribute to the deep flavours. Serve with fresh berries.

Stout (or dark) beer	1 cup	250 mL
Fancy (mild) molasses	2/3 cup	150 mL
Large eggs	3	3
Brown sugar, packed	1 cup	250 mL
Unsweetened applesauce	2/3 cup	150 mL
Cooking oil	1/2 cup	125 mL
All-purpose flour	2 1/2 cups	625 mL
Cocoa, sifted if lumpy	1/4 cup	60 mL
Ground ginger	2 tbsp.	30 mL
Baking powder	1 1/2 tsp.	7 mL
Baking soda	1 tsp.	5 mL
Ground cinnamon	1 tsp.	5 mL
Ground allspice	1/2 tsp.	2 mL
Ground nutmeg	1/2 tsp.	2 mL
Salt	1/2 tsp.	2 mL
Icing (confectioner's) sugar	1 tbsp.	15 mL

Combine beer and molasses in a medium saucepan on medium heat and bring to a boil. Carefully transfer mixture to a medium bowl. Let stand for about 1 hour, stirring occasionally, until cooled to room temperature.

Add next 4 ingredients. Beat until brown sugar is dissolved.

Combine next 9 ingredients in a large bowl and make a well in centre. Add beer mixture to well and beat until smooth. Spread evenly in a greased 12 cup (3 L) Bundt pan. Bake in 350°F (175°C) oven for about 45 minutes until a wooden pick inserted in centre comes out clean. Let stand in pan on a wire rack for 10 minutes. Invert onto wire rack to cool completely.

Dust with icing sugar. Cuts into 16 pieces.

Spiced Rum Pear Cake

Sweet pears and colourful cherries make this moist spice cake a simple yet delicious dessert that will make any get-together special.

Butter (or hard margarine)	1/4 cup	60 mL
Brown sugar, packed	1/4 cup	60 mL
Diced peeled pear	2 cups	500 mL
Chopped dried cherries	1/4 cup	60 mL
Butter (or hard margarine), softened	1/3 cup	75 mL
Brown sugar, packed	2/3 cup	150 mL
Large eggs	2	2
Sour cream	1/2 cup	125 mL
Spiced rum (or orange juice)	2 tbsp.	30 mL
Grated orange zest, (see Tip, page 116)	1/2 tsp.	2 mL
Vanilla extract	1/2 tsp.	2 mL
All-purpose flour	1 1/4 cups	300 mL
Baking powder	1/2 tsp.	2 mL
Baking soda	1/4 tsp.	1 mL
Ground cinnamon	1/4 tsp.	1 mL
Salt	1/4 tsp.	1 mL

Melt butter in a medium saucepan on medium heat. Add first amount of brown sugar. Heat, stirring, until brown sugar is dissolved.

Add pear and cherries. Cook for about 5 minutes, stirring often, until pear is tender.

Beat second amount of butter and second amount of brown sugar in a large bowl until light and fluffy.

Add eggs, 1 at a time, beating well after each addition. Add next 4 ingredients. Beat well.

Combine remaining 5 ingredients in a medium bowl. Add to butter mixture in 2 additions, mixing well after each addition until no dry flour remains. Add pear mixture and stir until just combined. Spread in a greased 9 inch (23 cm) round pan. Bake in 350°F (175°C) oven for about 45 minutes until a wooden pick inserted in centre comes out clean. Let stand in pan on a wire rack until cool. Cuts into 12 wedges.

Blueberry Lemon Layer Cake

This lovely cake is sweet yet tangy. The lemon cream cheese icing elevates this cake from delicious to outstanding. You'll need about 3 medium lemons for this recipe.

Butter (or hard margarine), softened	1 cup	250 mL
Granulated sugar	1 cup	250 mL
Brown sugar, packed	1/2 cup	125 mL
Large eggs	4	4
Vanilla extract	2 tsp.	10 mL
All-purpose flour	3 cups	750 mL
Baking powder	1 tbsp.	15 mL
Salt	1/2 tsp.	2 mL
Buttermilk (or soured milk, see Tip, page 68)	1 cup	250 mL
Lemon juice	1/2 cup	125 mL
Grated lemon zest	1 tbsp.	15 mL
Fresh (or frozen) blueberries	1 1/2 cups	375 mL
All-purpose flour	1 tbsp.	15 mL
LEMON CREAM CHEESE ICING		
Cream cheese, softened	12 oz.	340 g
Butter (or hard margarine), softened	1/2 cup	125 mL
Icing (confectioner's) sugar	4 1/2 cups	1.1 L
Grated lemon zest (see Tip, page 116)	1 tsp.	5 mL
Lemon juice	1 tbsp.	15 mL
Milk	2 tbsp.	30 mL
Vanilla extract	1 tsp.	5 mL

Cream first amount of butter and both sugars in a large bowl. Add eggs, 1 at a time, beating well after each addition. Add vanilla. Beat until smooth.

Combine next 3 ingredients in a medium bowl. Gradually stir into butter mixture, stirring until just combined. Add next 3 ingredients, stirring until just combined.

Combine blueberries and remaining flour in a small bowl. Fold into batter. Do not overmix. Divide evenly among 3 greased 9 inch (23 cm) round pans. Bake in 350°F (175°C) oven for about 20 minutes, until a wooden pick inserted in centre comes out clean. Set aside to cool.

For the icing, beat cream cheese and remaining butter in a large bowl until light and fluffy. Add next 3 ingredients and beat on low until combined. Increase speed to medium and beat until creamy.

Add milk and vanilla and beat until light and fluffy. Place 1 cake on a serving plate. If cake is too round on top, use a serrated knife to trim top. Spread with icing. Repeat with remaining cakes and icing. Spread icing on top and sides of cake. Cuts into 16 wedges.

Apple Carrot Cake

Using applesauce instead of cooking oil cuts calories and boosts flavour. Toss the apple-slice garnish with lemon juice to prevent browning. Wrap leftovers well to maintain moisture.

All-purpose flour	1 1/2 cups	375 mL
Whole-wheat flour	1/2 cup	125 mL
Baking soda	2 tsp.	10 mL
Ground cinnamon	1 1/2 tsp.	7 mL
Salt	1 tsp.	5 mL
Ground nutmeg	1/2 tsp.	2 mL
Large eggs	4	4
Grated carrot	2 cups	500 mL
Grated peeled cooking apple (such as McIntosh)	1 1/2 cups	375 mL
Applesauce	1 cup	250 mL
Golden raisins	1 cup	250 mL
Granulated sugar	1 cup	250 mL
APPLE CREAM ICING		
Icing (confectioner's) sugar	1 cup	250 mL
Light cream cheese, softened	4 oz.	113 g
Hard margarine (or butter), softened	1/4 cup	60 mL
Frozen concentrated apple juice	2 tbsp.	30 mL

Apple slices, for garnish

Combine first 6 ingredients in a large bowl. Make a well in centre.

Combine next 6 ingredients in a separate large bowl. Add to well and stir until just moistened. Spread in a greased 9 x 13 inch (23 x 33 cm) pan. Bake in 350°F (175°C) oven for about 45 minutes until a wooden pick inserted in centre comes out clean. Set aside to cool completely.

For the icing, beat next 4 ingredients in a medium bowl on medium until smooth. Spread over cake in pan.

Garnish with apple slices. Cuts into 12 pieces.

Cherry Snack Cake

This fun, rosy-coloured cake is loaded with cherries and chocolate. The dusting of icing sugar gives it a lovely presentation.

Butter (or hard margarine), softened	1/2 cup	125 mL
Granulated sugar	1 cup	250 mL
Large eggs	2	2
Vanilla extract	1 tsp.	5 mL
Semi-sweet baking chocolate, grated	1 oz.	28 g
Chopped maraschino cherries	1/4 cup	60 mL
All-purpose flour	1 1/2 cups	375 mL
Baking powder	1 1/2 tsp.	7 mL
Salt	1/4 tsp.	1 mL
Maraschino cherry syrup	1/4 cup	60 mL

Icing (confectioner's) sugar, for dusting

Cream butter and sugar in a large bowl. Add eggs, 1 at a time, beating well after each addition.

Stir in vanilla, chocolate and cherries.

Combine flour, baking powder and salt in a small bowl.

Add flour mixture to butter mixture in 3 additions, alternating with cherry syrup in 2 additions, beginning and ending with flour mixture. Spread in a greased 9 x 9 inch (23 x 23 cm) pan. Bake in 350°F (175°C) oven for about 35 minutes until a wooden pick inserted in centre comes out clean. Set aside to cool completely.

Dust individual servings with icing sugar. Cuts into 9 pieces as a dessert or 12 pieces as a snack.

Sticky Date Pudding

This sticky, cake-like pudding with a delicious buttery caramel sauce is based on the ever-popular English sticky toffee pudding. Serve warm.

Water	1 1/3 cups	325 mL
Seeded dates, coarsely chopped	1 1/3 cups	325 mL
Baking soda	1 tsp.	5 mL
Butter (or hard margarine), softened	1/3 cup	75 mL
Brown sugar, packed	3/4 cup	175 mL
Large eggs	2	2
All-purpose flour	1 cup	250 mL
Baking powder	2 tsp.	10 mL
Ground cinnamon	1 tsp.	5 mL
WARM CARAMEL SAUCE		
Whipping cream	1/2 cup	125 mL
Butter (or hard margarine)	1/2 cup	125 mL
Brown sugar, packed	1/2 cup	125 mL

Bring water to a boil in a medium saucepan. Stir in dates and remove from heat. Stir in baking soda and let stand for 10 minutes. Stir again and pour into a large bowl.

Add next 6 ingredients. Beat until well combined. Pour into a greased 8 inch (20 cm) springform pan lined with parchment paper. Bake in 350°F (175°C) oven for 50 to 55 minutes until a wooden pick inserted in centre comes out clean. Let stand in pan for 10 minutes before turning out onto a wire rack to cool.

For the sauce, combine whipping cream and remaining butter and brown sugar in a large saucepan on medium heat. Cook, stirring, for 3 to 5 minutes until butter is melted. Bring to a boil and cook, without stirring, for about 5 minutes until slightly thickened. Serve drizzled over cake. Cuts into 8 wedges.

Figgy Orange Cake

This buttery spice cake is filled with the appealing texture of figs. It is delicious as-is or dressed with Orange Glaze (see page 100). You can also garnish the cake with fresh figs for an unexpected look.

Granulated sugar	1 cup	250 mL
Brown sugar, packed	1/2 cup	125 mL
Butter (or hard margarine), softened	1/2 cup	125 mL
Large eggs	3	3
Vanilla extract	1 tsp.	5 mL
All-purpose flour	2 1/2 cups	625 mL
Baking powder	1 tsp.	5 mL
Baking soda	1 tsp.	5 mL
Ground cinnamon	1/2 tsp.	2 mL
Ground ginger	1/2 tsp.	2 mL
Salt	1/2 tsp.	2 mL
Orange juice	1 1/4 cups	300 mL
Chopped dried figs	1 cup	250 mL
Grated orange zest (see Tip, page 116)	2 tsp.	10 mL

Beat sugar, brown sugar and butter in a large bowl until light and fluffy. Add eggs, 1 at a time, beating well after each addition. Stir in vanilla.

Combine next 6 ingredients in a medium bowl. Add flour mixture to butter mixture in 3 additions, alternating with first amount of orange juice in 2 additions, stirring well after each addition until just combined.

Stir in figs and orange zest. Grease and flour a 10 inch (25 cm) angel food tube pan with a removable bottom. Spread batter in prepared pan. Bake in 350°F (175°C) oven for about 1 hour until a wooden pick inserted in centre of cake comes out clean. Let stand in pan on a wire rack for 30 minutes. Run a knife around edge of pan to loosen cake. Remove bottom of pan with cake. Run knife around bottom and centre tube of pan to loosen cake. Invert cake onto a serving plate. Set aside to cool. Cuts into 16 pieces.

Red Velvet Cake

Red velvet cake is more than just a chocolate cake with red food colouring added. Original red velvet recipes did not contain any food colouring; a chemical reaction between the cocoa, buttermilk and vinegar gave the cake a natural reddish colour. Most recipes today call for food colouring to make the cake a more vibrant red.

All-purpose flour	2 1/2 cups	625 mL
Cocoa	1 tsp.	5 mL
Salt	1 tsp.	5 mL
Butter (or hard margarine), softened	1/2 cup	125 mL
Granulated sugar	1 1/2 cups	375 mL
Large eggs	2	2
Red food coloring paste	2 tsp.	10 mL
Vanilla extract	1 tsp.	5 mL
Buttermilk	1 cup	250 mL
Baking soda	1 tsp.	5 mL
White vinegar	1 tsp.	5 mL
VELVETY CREAM CHEESE ICING		
Milk	2 cups	500 mL
All-purpose flour	1/4 cup	60 mL
Butter (or hard margarine), softened	2 cups	500 mL
Granulated sugar	2 cups	500 mL
Vanilla extract	2 tsp.	10 mL

Combine flour, cocoa and salt in a medium bowl.

Cream butter and first amount of sugar together in a large bowl. Add eggs, 1 at a time, beating well after each addition. Add food coloring and first amount of vanilla. Add flour mixture alternately with buttermilk, beginning and ending with flour mixture.

Mix baking soda into vinegar in a small cup and stir into batter. Divide among 3 greased 9 inch (23 cm) round cake pans. Bake in 350°F (175°C) oven for 25 to 30 minutes until a wooden pick inserted in center comes out clean. Let stand for 10 minutes before turning out onto racks to cool.

For the icing, gradually whisk milk into flour in a small saucepan until smooth. Heat, stirring, until boiling and thickened. Cool completely.

Beat second amount of butter on high. Gradually add remaining sugar until completely incorporated. Add remaining vanilla and milk mixture. Beat on high until light and fluffy. Spread between layers and on top and sides of cake. Cuts into 16 pieces.

Peanut Butter Layer Cake

We've chosen a mild peanut butter icing with a dusting of cocoa for this superb, moist cake but it would also be delicious iced with Simple Chocolate Frosting (see page 52) or Chocolate Ganache (see page 118).

Butter (or soft margarine), softened	1/2 cup	125 mL
Smooth peanut butter	1/2 cup	125 mL
Brown sugar, packed	1 1/2 cups	375 mL
Large eggs	2	2
Vanilla extract	1 tsp.	5 mL
All-purpose flour	2 cups	500 mL
Baking powder	2 1/2 tsp.	12 mL
Milk	1 cup	250 mL
PEANUT BUTTER ICING		
Butter (or soft margarine), softened	1/4 cup	60 mL
Smooth peanut butter	1/4 cup	60 mL
Vanilla	1/2 tsp.	2 mL
Salt	1/8 tsp.	0.5 mL
Icing (confectioner's) sugar	2 cups	500 mL
Milk	3 tbsp.	45 mL
Cocoa, for dusting		

Cream first 2 ingredients together in a mixing bowl. Add brown sugar and beat until light and fluffy. Add eggs, 1 at a time, beating well after each addition. Beat in vanilla.

Combine flour and baking powder in a small bowl.

Add flour to butter mixture in 3 parts alternately with milk in 2 parts, beginning and ending with flour. Spread evenly in 2 greased 8 inch (20 cm) round pans. Bake in 350°F (175°C) oven for 30 to 35 minutes until a wooden pick inserted in centre comes out clean. Let stand in pans for 10 minutes before removing to racks to cool completely.

For the icing, combine remaining 6 ingredients in a mixing bowl and beat until smooth. Spread between layers and on top and sides of cake. Dust with cocoa. Cuts into 12 wedges.

Fruitcake

Anyone who thinks fruitcake is dry and unappealing hasn't tried this cake. Nicely spiced with undertones of coffee and molasses, this cake has a little something for everyone.

Raisins	2 cups	500 mL
Chopped citron	1 cup	250 mL
Slivered almonds, toasted (see Tip, page 148)	1 cup	250 mL
Holiday fruit mix, with peel	1 cup	250 mL
Glazed cherries, chopped	1/4 cup	60 mL
All-purpose flour	1/3 cup	75 mL
Butter (or hard margarine), softened	1 cup	250 mL
Granulated sugar	1 1/2 cups	375 mL
Large eggs	4	4
Fancy molasses	1/2 cup	125 mL
Prepared coffee	1/2 cup	125 mL
All-purpose flour	3 cups	750 mL
Ground cinnamon	1 tsp.	5 mL
Ground allspice	1/2 tsp.	2 mL
Ground cloves	1/2 tsp.	2 mL
Baking soda	1 tsp.	5 mL

Measure first 6 ingredients into a medium bowl. Toss well to coat with flour.

Cream butter and sugar together in a large bowl. Add eggs, 1 at a time, beating well after each addition. Mix in molasses and prepared coffee.

Stir remaining 5 ingredients together in a separate medium bowl. Add to coffee mixture and stir just to moisten. Gently stir in fruit mixture. Line two 9 x 5 x 3 inch (23 x 12.5 x 7.5 cm) loaf pans with parchment paper. Divide dough between pans. Place a separate pan filled with about 1 inch (2.5 cm) water on bottom rack in oven. Bake cakes on center rack in 275°F (140°C) oven for about 2 hours and 50 minutes until a wooden pick inserted in center comes out clean. Let stand for 10 minutes before removing to a rack to cool. Makes 2 cakes. Each cake cuts into 20 pieces, for a total of 40 pieces.

Sacher Torte

This classic Austrian torte is a wonderful combination of chocolate and apricot flavours. Serve with whipped cream for an extra special treat.

Semi-sweet baking chocolate, cut up	5 oz.	140 g
Butter (or hard margarine)	1 tbsp.	15 mL
Butter (or hard margarine), softened	1/2 cup	125 mL
Granulated sugar	1/2 cup	125 mL
Egg yolks (large)	5	5
Vanilla extract	1 tsp.	5 mL
Cocoa, sifted	2 tbsp.	30 mL
All-purpose flour	3/4 cup	175 mL
Salt	1/4 tsp.	1 mL
Egg whites (large), room temperature	5	5
Apricot jam, heated and sieved	1 cup	250 mL

Chocolate Ganache, page 118

Melt chocolate and first amount of butter in a medium saucepan on low, stirring constantly, until smooth (see Tip, page 140). Cool to room temperature.

Cream second amount of butter and sugar in a medium bowl. Beat in egg yolks and vanilla until light and fluffy. Beat in chocolate.

Sift cocoa into flour and salt in a small bowl. Stir into chocolate mixture.

Beat egg whites with clean beaters in a large bowl until stiff. Fold into chocolate mixture in 4 additions. Turn into a greased 9 inch (23 cm) springform pan. Bake in 350°F (175°C) oven for about 35 minutes until a wooden pick inserted in center comes out clean. Set aside to cool.

Cut cake into 2 layers. Spread bottom layer with scant 1/2 cup (125 mL) apricot jam. Add top layer. Spread remaining jam over top and sides. Let stand 1 hour or more to dry slightly.

Pour ganache over top and down sides of cake. Cuts into 12 wedges.

Hazelnut Torte

With its heady combination of chocolate, hazelnut and coffee, this torte is as elegant as it is delicious. Perfect for any special occasion! Garnish with toasted hazelnuts for a pretty presentation.

Cake flour	2 cups	500 mL
Baking powder	2 tsp.	10 mL
Salt	1/2 tsp.	2 mL
Egg yolks (large)	6	6
Cooking oil	1/2 cup	125 mL
Water	1/2 cup	125 mL
Granulated sugar	1 cup	250 mL
Egg whites (large)	6	6
Hazelnuts, chopped and toasted (see Tip, page 148)	1 cup	250 mL
Strong brewed coffee, cooled	1/4 cup	60 mL
Whipping cream	1 cup	250 mL
Bittersweet chocolate, chopped	6 oz.	170 g
Jar of chocolate hazelnut spread (14 oz., 400 g)	1	1

Combine flour, baking powder and salt in a bowl and set aside.

In a large mixing bowl, beat egg yolks, oil, water and sugar with an electric mixer on medium speed for 5 minutes, scraping bowl occasionally. Fold in flour mixture.

In another large mixing bowl, beat egg whites with an electric mixer on medium to high speed until soft peaks form. Gently fold about 1 cup (250 mL) of egg white mixture into egg yolk mixture. Fold remaining egg yolk mixture into remaining egg white mixture. Fold in chopped hazelnuts. Grease and lightly flour two 9-inch (23 cm) springform pans. Spoon batter evenly into prepared pans. Bake in 350°F (175°C) oven for 20 minutes or until a toothpick inserted in centre comes out clean.

Immediately poke holes in cakes with a toothpick and drizzle coffee evenly over. Let stand on wire racks for 10 minutes before removing from pans. Set aside to cool completely. Slice cooled cakes in half horizontally.

In a medium saucepan, heat whipping cream to a simmer. Remove from heat and add bittersweet chocolate, stirring until melted. Reserve 1/4 cup (60 mL) of chocolate mixture for drizzling; cover and set aside.

Cool remaining chocolate mixture to room temperature, about an hour. Transfer mixture to a medium bowl and beat with an electric mixer on medium speed until thickened, about 3 minutes. Spread chocolate filling evenly on 3 cake layers.

Frost top and sides with chocolate hazelnut spread. Drizzle reserved chocolate on top. Cuts into 12 slices.

Last Minute Torte

Use a prepared pound cake for this torte if you are short on time. If you are not in a time crunch, try using one of the pound cakes earlier in this book, such as the Old Time Pound Cake (see page 28) or White Chocolate Pound Cake (see page 30). These cakes are a little larger than most store bought frozen pound cakes, though, so you may consider making a little more icing.

FUDGE ICING		
Semisweet chocolate chips	1 cup	250 mL
Sour cream	1 cup	250 mL
Prepared pound cake (about 14 oz, 390 g)	1	1
Sliced or slivered almonds, toasted (see Tip, page 148)	1 cup	250 mL

For the icing, heat chocolate chips and sour cream in a medium saucepan over hot (not boiling) water, stirring constantly until smooth (see Tip, page 140). Set aside to cool to room temperature.

Cut pound cake into 5 layers (see Tip, below).

Spread 1/4 cup (60 mL) icing over top of each layer. Sprinkle each layer with 1/6 of almonds, pressing down lightly to ensure they stick. Assemble layers as you go. Spread remaining icing over sides. Press remaining almonds on sides. Cuts into 10 slices.

Tip: It is easiest to cut the cake into layers if it is partially frozen.

Pumpkin Dessert

Almost like pumpkin pie—but without the crust. A cake mix makes this easy and fast—it takes only 20 minutes to assemble. Add a small dollop of ice cream for that delightful warm/cold contrast.

Large eggs	4	4
Granulated sugar	1 1/4 cups	300 mL
Cans of pure pumpkin (no spices), 14 oz., 398 mL, each	2	2
Ground cinnamon	1 1/2 tsp.	7 mL
Ground ginger	1 tsp.	5 mL
Salt	1 tsp.	5 mL
Ground cloves	1/2 tsp.	2 mL
Ground nutmeg	1/2 tsp.	2 mL
Evaporated milk (or half-and-half cream)	1 1/2 cups	375 mL
Butter (or hard margarine)	1/2 cup	125 mL
Box of yellow cake mix (2 layer size)	1	1
Vanilla ice cream (optional)		

Beat eggs in a medium bowl until frothy. Add sugar and beat until thick and pale.

Add next 6 ingredients and beat well.

Add evaporated milk and beat on low until well combined. Pour into a greased 9 x 13 inch (23 x 33 cm) pan.

In a large bowl, cut butter into cake mix until mixture resembles coarse crumbs. Sprinkle over pumpkin mixture. Bake in 350°F (175°C) oven for 1 1/2 hours until knife inserted in centre comes out clean.

Serve warm with ice cream. Cuts into 18 squares.

Pineapple Kuchen

This kuchen (KOO-khen) is a not-too-sweet dessert that's easy on the waistline.

All-purpose flour	1/2 cup	125 mL
Yellow cornmeal	1/2 cup	125 mL
Quick-cooking rolled oats	1/3 cup	75 mL
Baking powder	1 tsp.	5 mL
Baking soda	1/8 tsp.	0.5 mL
Ground cinnamon	1/8 tsp.	0.5 mL
Large egg, fork-beaten	1	1
Non-fat plain yogurt	1/2 cup	125 mL
Brown sugar, packed	1/4 cup	60 mL
Butter (or hard margarine), melted	2 tbsp.	30 mL
Can of pineapple tidbits (14 oz., 398 mL), drained	1	1
Chopped pecans	2 tbsp.	30 mL
Liquid honey, warmed	2 tbsp.	30 mL

Combine first 6 ingredients in a medium bowl.

Combine next 4 ingredients in a small bowl. Add to dry ingredients and stir until just moistened. Transfer to a greased 9 inch (23 cm) glass pie plate.

Scatter pineapple and pecans over top and press down lightly to make sure they stick. Drizzle with honey. Bake in 350°F (175°C) oven for 25 minutes until wooden pick inserted in centre comes out clean. Serve warm. Cuts into 8 wedges.

Harvey Wallbanger Cake

The key to this cake, like the cocktail it takes its name from, is the Galliano liqueur. The alcohol bakes out, but the flavour remains. If you prefer not to use the glaze, you can top this moist cake with a dusting of icing sugar.

Yellow cake mix (2 layer size)	1	1
Instant vanilla pudding mix, 4 serving size	1	1
Orange juice	2/3 cup	150 mL
Vodka	1/4 cup	60 mL
Galliano liqueur	1/4 cup	60 mL
Cooking oil	1/2 cup	125 mL
Large eggs	4	4
ORANGE GLAZE		
Icing (confectioner's) sugar	1 cup	250 mL
Orange juice	3 tbsp.	45 mL

Combine first 7 ingredients in a large mixing bowl and beat on medium speed until smooth, about 2 minutes. Turn into a 12 cup (3 L) Bundt pan. Bake in 350°F (175°C) oven for about 45 minutes until a wooden pick inserted in centre comes out clean. Let stand 15 to 30 minutes. Remove from pan onto a plate and set aside to cool.

For the glaze, stir icing sugar and second amount of orange juice in a separate medium bowl until smooth. Drizzle over top of cake, allowing glaze to flow down sides. Cuts into 16 pieces.

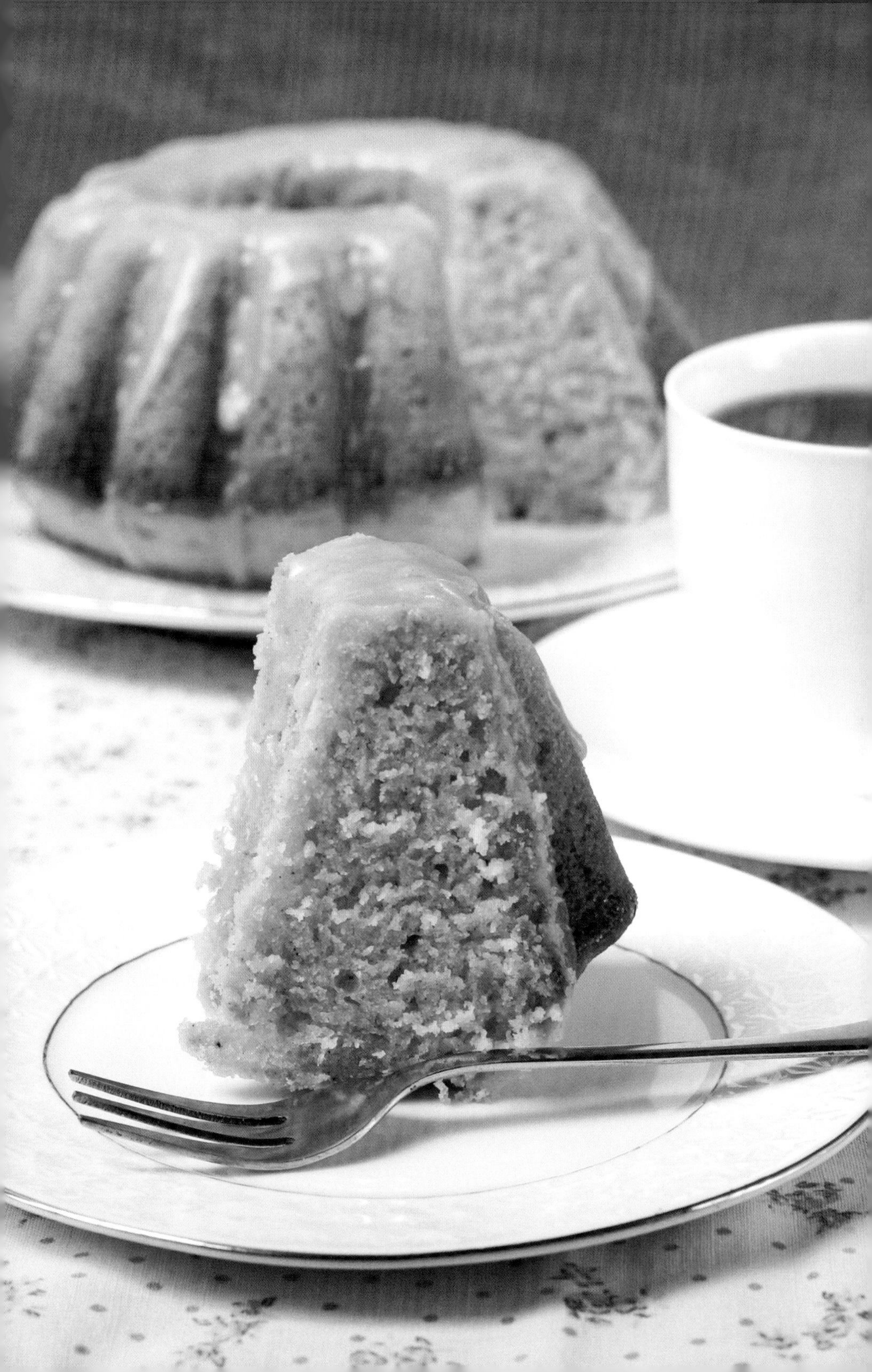

Black Forest Decadence

This cake is a real showpiece. Chocolate layers are filled with cherry cream and topped with a rich chocolate glaze. Top whipped cream garnish with stemmed maraschino cherries for an attractive presentation.

Dark chocolate cake mix (2 layer size)	1	1
Whipping cream (or 4 cups, 1 L, whipped topping)	2 cups	500 mL
Icing (confectioner's) sugar	1 tbsp.	15 mL
Can of cherry pie filling (19 oz., 540 mL)	1	1
CHOCOLATE GLAZE		
Semisweet baking chocolate, cut up	6 oz.	170 g
Light cream (half-and-half)	1/2 cup	125 mL

Prepare cake according to package directions and bake in 2 greased 9 inch (23 cm) round layer pans. Set aside to cool completely. Split each cake in half to make 4 layers.

Beat whipping cream and icing sugar in a large bowl until stiff. Reserve 1 cup (250 mL) for garnish.

Fold pie filling into remaining whipped cream. Spread 1/3 of cherry cream mixture over each of 3 layers, stacking as each is spread. Add fourth layer to top.

For the glaze, melt chocolate with light cream in a medium saucepan on low heat, stirring constantly, until smooth (see Tip, page 140). Set pan in cold water. Whisk until cooled enough to be slightly pourable. Drizzle over top of cake, allowing some to run down sides. Chill. Garnish with reserved whipped cream. Cuts into 16 wedges.

Cheery Cherry Cupcakes

These moist, cherry-flavoured cupcakes are loaded with crunchy pecans and chewy cherries.

Butter (or hard margarine), softened	1/2 cup	125 mL
Brown sugar, packed	1 cup	250 mL
Granulated sugar	1/4 cup	60 mL
Large eggs, fork-beaten	2	2
Almond extract	1/2 tsp.	2 mL
Apple juice	1/4 cup	60 mL
All-purpose flour	1 2/3 cups	400 mL
Baking powder	1 tsp.	5 mL
Salt	1/2 tsp.	2 mL
Chopped pecans	1/3 cup	75 mL
Chopped glazed cherries	1/2 cup	125 mL
CREAM CHEESE ICING		
Cream cheese, softened	4 oz.	125 g
Butter (or hard margarine)	1/4 cup	60 mL
Vanilla extract	1 tsp.	5 mL
Icing (confectioner's) sugar	2 cups	500 mL

Beat first 6 ingredients together in a large bowl until well combined.

Combine flour, baking powder and salt in a medium bowl. Add to butter mixture, stirring until no dry flour remains.

Sprinkle 1 tsp. (5 mL) pecans and 2 tsp. (10 mL) cherries into each of 12 greased muffin cups. Spoon batter over top. Bake in 400°F (200°C) oven for 18 to 20 minutes until a wooden pick inserted in centre comes out clean. Let stand in pan for 5 minutes before turning out onto a wire rack to cool.

For the icing, beat cream cheese, second amount of butter and vanilla. Gradually add in icing sugar, beating until light and fluffy. Spread over cupcakes. Makes 12 cupcakes.

Pineapple Upside-down Cupcakes

Cinnamon-flecked pineapple dresses up a simple white cupcake. A perfect light dessert.

Can of crushed pineapple or tidbits (14 oz., 398 mL), drained	1	1
Butter (or hard margarine), softened	1/4 cup	60 mL
Brown sugar, packed	1/2 cup	125 mL
Ground cinnamon	1 tsp.	5 mL
Red glazed cherries, cut in half	6	6
Large egg	1	1
Granulated sugar	2 tbsp.	30 mL
Butter (or hard margarine), softened	1/4 cup	60 mL
Milk	1 cup	250 mL
All-purpose flour	2 cups	500 mL
Baking powder	1 tbsp.	15 mL
Salt	1/2 tsp.	2 mL

Combine first 4 ingredients in a medium bowl. Place 1 cherry half in bottom of each greased muffin cup. Divide mixture evenly and spoon around cherry.

Beat egg, sugar and second amount of butter in a small bowl. Beat in milk.

Combine flour, baking powder and salt in a large bowl and make a well in centre. Pour milk mixture into well and stir until just moistened. Spoon onto pineapple mixture in muffin cups, dividing batter evenly among cups. Bake in 400°F (200°C) oven for about 18 minutes until a wooden pick inserted in centre comes out clean. Invert immediately onto a wire rack to cool. There will be some stickiness on bottom. Makes 12 cupcakes.

Blueberry Little Cakes

The perfect combination: blueberry and lemon. These rich and cakey treats will become an all-time favourite. We've garnished them with lemon zest and mint leaves as well as fresh blueberries to make them extra pretty.

Butter (or hard margarine)	3/4 cup	175 mL
Ground almonds	1 cup	250 mL
Egg whites (large), fork-beaten	6	6
Icing (confectioner's) sugar	1 1/2 cups	375 mL
All-purpose flour	1/2 cup	125 mL
Fresh blueberries	1 cup	250 mL
Finely grated lemon zest	2 tsp.	10 mL
WHIPPED CREAM FROSTING		
Whipping cream	1 1/4 cups	300 mL
Granulated sugar	2 tbsp.	30 mL
Fresh blueberries, for garnish		

Melt butter in a large saucepan.

Add next 6 ingredients and stir until just combined. Grease 12 muffin cups with cooking spray or line with paper liners. Fill cups 3/4 full. Bake in 375°F (190°C) oven for about 25 minutes until a wooden pick inserted in centre comes out clean. Let stand in pan for 10 minutes before removing to a wire rack to cool.

For the frosting, beat whipping cream and sugar in a small bowl until stiff peaks form. Chill for about 30 minutes. Spread over cupcakes. Garnish with blueberries. Makes 12 cupcakes.

Boston Cream Cupcakes

It's time you try our cupcake version of the classic Boston cream pie! Garnish with a cherry for a lovely presentation.

Ingredient	Imperial	Metric
All-purpose flour	1 1/2 cups	375 mL
Granulated sugar	1 cup	250 mL
Baking powder	1/2 tsp.	2 mL
Baking soda	1/4 tsp.	1 mL
Salt	1/2 tsp.	2 mL
Butter (or hard margarine)	1/2 cup	125 mL
Water	1/2 cup	125 mL
Large egg	1	1
Milk	1/4 cup	60 mL
Vanilla extract	1 tsp.	5 mL
Whipping cream	3/4 cup	175 mL
Instant vanilla pudding powder	1 tbsp.	15 mL
Whipping cream	1/4 cup	60 mL
Semi-sweet chocolate chips	1/2 cup	125 mL

Combine first 5 ingredients in large bowl. Set aside.

Heat butter and water in a small saucepan on medium, stirring constantly, until mixture comes to a boil. Add to flour mixture. Stir until combined.

Whisk next 3 ingredients in a small bowl. Add to butter mixture and whisk until smooth. Fill 12 paper-lined muffin cups 3/4 full. Bake in 350°F (175°C) oven for about 18 minutes until a wooden pick inserted in centre comes out clean. Let stand in pan for 10 minutes before removing to wire racks to cool completely. Remove paper liners.

Beat first amount of whipping cream and pudding powder in a medium bowl until soft peaks form. Cut cupcakes in half horizontally and spread pudding mixture on bottom halves. Cover with tops.

Heat second amount of whipping cream in a small saucepan on medium until hot, but not boiling. Remove from heat. Add chocolate chips and stir until smooth. Spread over tops of cupcakes. Makes 12 cupcakes.

Mini Coconut Cupcakes

Don't let the small size fool you. These charming cupcakes pack a coconutty punch! For the best results, make sure all the ingredients are at room temperature.

Butter (or hard margarine), softened	1/2 cup	125 mL
Granulated sugar	1 cup	250 mL
Large eggs	2	2
All-purpose flour	1 1/2 cups	375 mL
Baking powder	1 tbsp.	15 mL
Medium coconut	1/2 cup	125 mL
Sour cream	1 cup	250 mL
Milk	1/3 cup	75 mL
COCONUT ICING		
Icing sugar	2 cups	500 mL
Butter (or hard margarine), melted	3 tbsp.	45 mL
Milk	2 tbsp.	30 mL
Coconut extract	1/2 tsp.	2 mL
Ribbon or flaked coconut, for garnish		

Beat first amount of butter and sugar in a large bowl until light and fluffy. Add eggs, one at a time, beating well after each addition.

Sift flour and baking powder into a medium bowl. Add to butter mixture. Stir in coconut. Fold in sour cream and milk. Fill greased mini muffin cups 3/4 full (see Tip, below). Bake in 350°F (175°C) oven for about 20 minutes until a wooden pick inserted in centre comes out clean. Let stand in pan for 10 minutes before removing to wire racks to cool completely.

For the icing, combine remaining 4 ingredients in a medium bowl. Spread over tops of cupcakes. Garnish with coconut. Makes 24 mini muffins.

Tip: To ensure even baking when you have empty muffin cups, fill empty cups with about 1/4 inch (6 mm) of water.

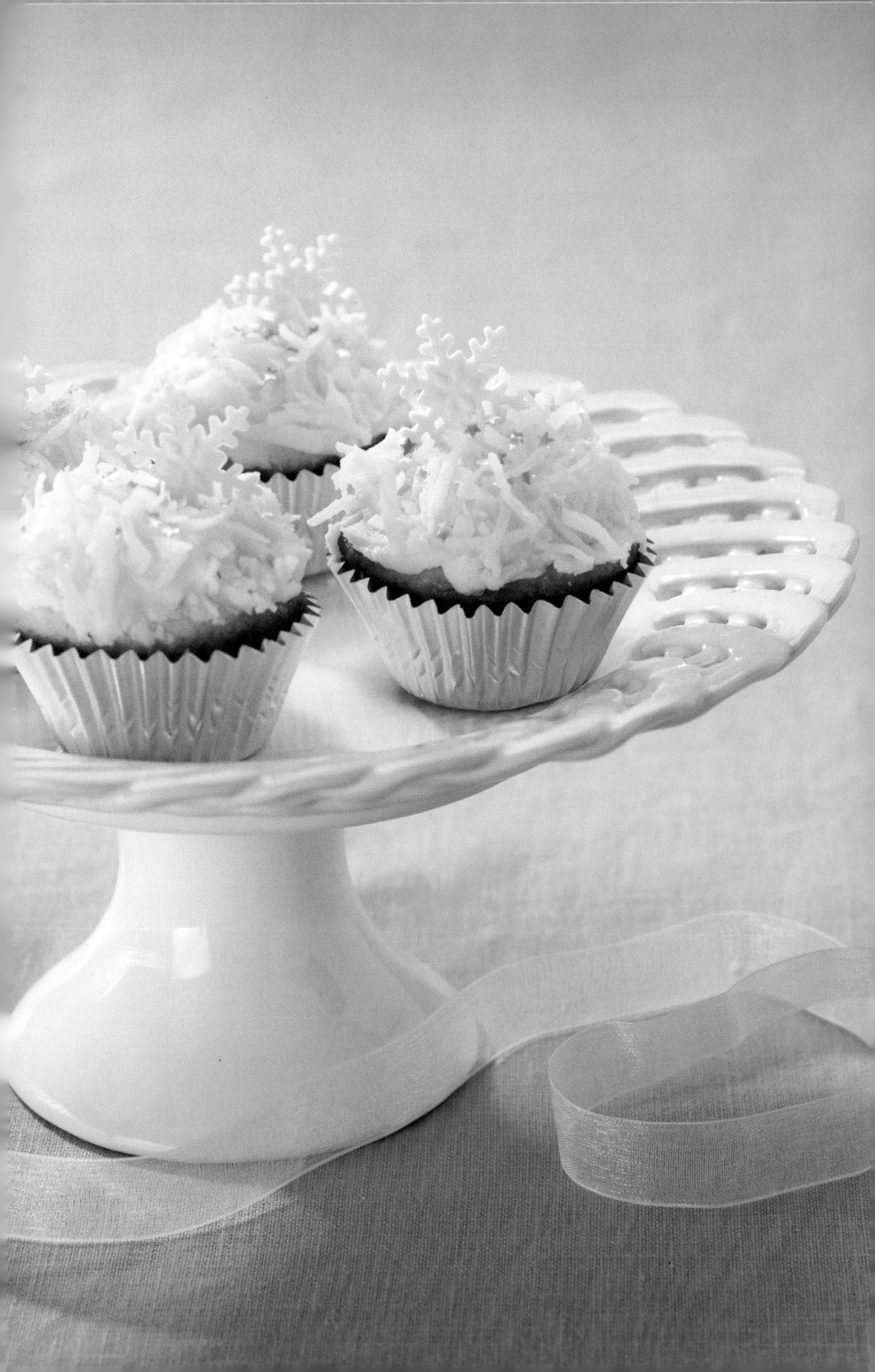

Brownie Cupcakes

To make these tasty cupcakes especially elegant, use stencils to dust the tops with icing sugar.

Semi-sweet baking chocolate, chopped	2 oz.	57 g
Butter (or hard margarine)	1/2 cup	125 mL
Brown sugar, packed	1 1/2 cups	375 mL
All-purpose flour	1 cup	250 mL
Large eggs, fork-beaten	2	2
Vanilla extract	1 tsp.	5 mL
Chopped pecans (or walnuts)	1/2 cup	125 mL
Salt	1/4 tsp.	1 mL
SIMPLE CHOCOLATE ICING		
Butter (or hard margarine), softened	3 tbsp.	45 mL
Icing (confectioner's) sugar	1 1/2 cups	375 mL
Cocoa, sifted if lumpy	1/3 cup	75 mL
Water, approximately	2 tbsp.	30 mL
Icing (confectioner's) sugar, for dusting		

Melt chocolate and butter in a saucepan on low heat, stirring often (see Tip, page 140). Remove from heat.

Add next 6 ingredients. Stir until just moistened. Fill greased muffin cups 3/4 full. Bake in 350°F (175°C) oven for 20 to 25 minutes until a wooden pick inserted in centre comes out clean. Let stand in pan for 10 minutes before removing to wire racks to cool completely.

For the icing, mix second amount of butter, icing sugar and cocoa in a small bowl. Add just enough water to make a barely pourable consistency. Spread on cooled cupcakes. Dust with icing sugar. Makes 12 cupcakes.

Orange Blossom Little Cakes

These delicately flavoured mini-cupcakes shyly steal the spotlight. The light orange blossom buttercream has lovely floral notes.

All-purpose flour	1 cup	250 mL
Granulated sugar	1/2 cup	125 mL
Grated orange zest (see Tip, below)	1 1/2 tsp.	7 mL
Baking powder	1 tsp.	5 mL
Salt	1/8 tsp.	0.5 mL
Butter, cut up and softened	1/2 cup	125 mL
Large egg	1	1
Whipping cream	1/4 cup	60 mL
Orange juice	2 tbsp.	30 mL
ORANGE BLOSSOM FROSTING		
Whipping cream	3/4 cup	175 mL
Instant vanilla pudding powder	2 tbsp.	30 mL
Orange blossom water	2 tsp.	10 mL

Combine first 5 ingredients in a mixing bowl. Add first amount of butter and beat until mixture is crumbly.

Combine next 3 ingredients and add to flour mixture. Beat for 1 minute until smooth. Line 24 mini-muffin cups with paper liners and fill with batter until 3/4 full (see Tip, page 112). Bake in a 350°F (175°C) oven for 12 minutes until a wooden pick inserted in centre comes out clean. Let stand in pan for 10 minutes before removing to wire racks to cool.

For the frosting, combine remaining 3 ingredients in a bowl and beat on high until stiff peaks form. Spoon into a small freezer bag with a small corner snipped off and pipe frosting onto cakes. Makes 24 mini cupcakes.

Tip: When a recipe calls for grated zest and juice, it's easier to grate the fruit first, then juice it. Be careful not to grate down to the pith the (white part of the peel), which is bitter and best avoided.

Orange blossom water is distilled water that has been flavoured with bitter orange flower blossoms. It is relatively new to the North American market but has been a part of Persian cuisine for ages. If you cannot find orange blossom water at your local supermarket, check a Persian or Middle Eastern grocery store.

Turtle Cheesecake

This scrumptious cheesecake is large enough for a group, but once you taste it, you'll heading back for seconds (or thirds; it's that good!). Even better, it can be made ahead and frozen.

All-purpose flour	1 1/2 cups	375 mL
Granulated sugar	3 tbsp.	45 mL
Butter (or hard margarine), cut up	3/4 cup	175 mL
Finely chopped pecans	3/4 cup	175 mL
Evaporated milk (or light cream)	3 tbsp.	45 mL
Caramels	32	32
Blocks of cream cheese, softened (8 oz., 250 g, each)	3	3
Brown sugar, packed	1 cup	250 mL
All-purpose flour	2 tbsp.	30 mL
Large eggs	3	3
Creamed cottage cheese, processed in a blender or sieved	1 cup	250 mL
Vanilla extract	1 1/2 tsp.	7 mL
Chopped pecans, toasted (see Tip, page 148)	1 cup	250 mL
Caramel (or butterscotch) ice cream topping	3 tbsp.	45 mL
CHOCOLATE GANACHE		
Whipping cream	1 cup	250 mL
Semi-sweet baking chocolate, chopped	7	7

For the crust, combine flour and first amount of sugar in a medium bowl. Cut in butter until mixture resembles coarse crumbs. Stir in pecans and press in bottom and 1 inch (2.5 cm) up side of greased 10 inch (25 cm) springform pan. Bake in 350°F (175°C) oven for 15 to 20 minutes until edge starts to brown. Let stand in pan on a wire rack for 10 minutes.

For the caramel layer, heat next 2 ingredients in a small saucepan on medium-low until caramels are melted. Pour over crust and spread evenly.

For the cheese layer, beat cream cheese and brown sugar in a large bowl until smooth. Beat in remaining flour. Add eggs, 1 at a time, beating after each addition until just combined. Beat in cottage cheese and vanilla on low until just combined. Pour over caramels and spread evenly. Bake in 350°F (175°C) oven for about 1 hour until centre is almost set. Run a knife around inside edge of pan to allow cheesecake to settle evenly. Let stand in pan on a wire rack set in a baking sheet with sides until cooled completely. Remove side of pan. Sprinkle pecans over top. Drizzle with caramel topping.

For the ganache, heat whipping cream in a heavy medium saucepan on medium-low until bubbles start to form around edge. Do not boil. Remove from heat. Stir in chocolate until mixture is smooth. Let stand for about 5 minutes to cool slightly before using. Pour over cheesecake, allowing it to drip down sides. Chill for at least 1 hour. Cuts into 16 wedges.

Pumpkin Caramel Cheesecake

Light, fluffy pumpkin filling rests atop a rich gingersnap crust, all drizzled with a caramel sauce spiked with bourbon.

Crushed gingersnaps (about 35)	1 1/2 cups	375 mL
Butter (or hard margarine), melted	1/3 cup	75 mL
Brown sugar, packed	2 tbsp.	30 mL
Envelope of unflavoured gelatin (1/4 oz., 7 g)	1	1
Water	3 tbsp.	45 mL
Block cream cheese, softened (8 oz., 250 g, each)	2	2
Canned pure pumpkin (no spices)	1/2 cup	125 mL
Sour cream	1/2 cup	125 mL
Brown sugar, packed	1/3 cup	75 mL
Ground ginger	1/2 tsp.	2 mL
CARAMEL BOURBON SAUCE		
Caramel (or butterscotch) ice cream topping	1/2 cup	125 mL
Bourbon whiskey	1 tbsp.	15 mL

Combine first 3 ingredients in a medium bowl. Press firmly in bottom of a greased 9 inch (23 cm) springform pan. Bake in 350°F (175°C) oven for 10 minutes. Set on a wire rack to cool.

Sprinkle gelatin over water in a small saucepan and let stand for 1 minute. Heat, stirring, on medium-low for about 1 minute until gelatin is dissolved. Remove from heat.

Beat next 5 ingredients in a large bowl until combined. Add gelatin mixture and beat until smooth. Spread evenly in crust. Chill, covered, for at least 3 hours until set.

Combine ice cream topping and bourbon in a small bowl. Drizzle over whole cake or individual wedges. Cuts into 12 wedges.

Upside-down Cheesecake

To make the heart-shaped pattern in the sauce, use an eyedropper filled with whipping cream to create dots at even intervals around the cake, then drag a toothpick in a continuous line around the plate. Decorate cakes with chocolate filigrees for an elegant touch.

Butter (or hard margarine)	1/3 cup	75 mL
Vanilla wafer crumbs	1 1/4 cups	300 mL
Hazelnuts (filberts), toasted (see Tip, page 148) and finely ground	1 cup	250 mL
Envelope of unflavoured gelatin (1/4 oz., 7 g)	1	1
Cold water	1/3 cup	75 mL
Block of cream cheese (8 oz., 250 g), softened	1	1
Sour cream	1 cup	250 mL
Granulated sugar	1/3 cup	75 mL
White baking chocolate, melted (see Tip, page 140)	6 oz.	170 g
Hazelnut liqueur	3 tbsp.	45 mL
Whipping cream	1/2 cup	125 mL
CHOCOLATE SAUCE		
Semi-sweet baking chocolate, chopped	4 oz.	113 g
Whipping cream	1/4 cup	60 mL
Butter (or hard margarine)	1 tbsp.	15 mL
Hazelnut liqueur	1 tbsp.	15 mL

For the crust, line bottom and sides of six 1 cup (250 mL) metal molds or ramekins with parchment (or waxed) paper. Melt butter in a medium saucepan on medium. Remove from heat. Stir in wafer crumbs and hazelnuts. Press firmly into bottom of prepared molds. Chill for 15 minutes.

For the filling, sprinkle gelatin over cold water in a small saucepan and let stand for 1 minute. Heat, stirring, on low until gelatin is dissolved. Set aside to cool.

Beat next 3 ingredients in a large bowl until smooth. Beat in gelatin mixture, white chocolate and liqueur.

Beat whipping cream in a small bowl until soft peaks form. Fold into cream cheese mixture. Spread evenly in molds. Chill, covered, for at least 6 hours or overnight.

For the sauce, heat next 3 ingredients in a small heavy saucepan on low, stirring often, until butter and chocolate are almost melted. Do not overheat. Remove from heat and stir until smooth. Stir in liqueur and let stand for 1 minute. Invert cheesecakes onto 6 plates. Spoon sauce around cheesecakes. Makes 6 cheesecakes.

Linzer Cheesecake

The popular linzer torte is recreated as a delicious cheesecake—perfectly emulated both in flavour and appearance.

Ground almonds	1 cup	250 mL
All-purpose flour	1/2 cup	125 mL
Ground cinnamon	1/2 tsp.	2 mL
Ground allspice	1/4 tsp.	1 mL
Salt	1/4 tsp.	1 mL
Butter (or hard margarine), softened	1/2 cup	125 mL
Brown sugar, packed	1/2 cup	125 mL
Large egg, fork-beaten	1	1
Block cream cheese (8 oz., 250 g, each), cut up and softened	2	2
Granulated sugar	1/4 cup	60 mL
All-purpose flour	3 tbsp.	45 mL
Large eggs, fork-beaten	3	3
Sour cream	1 cup	250 mL
Frozen concentrated raspberry (or mixed berry) cocktail, thawed	1/2 cup	125 mL
Almond extract	1 tsp.	5 mL
Raspberry jam	1/2 cup	125 mL
Sliced natural almonds, toasted (see Tip, page 148), finely chopped	1/2 cup	125 mL

Combine first 5 ingredients in a medium bowl.

Beat butter and brown sugar in a separate medium bowl until light and fluffy. Add egg and beat until smooth. Add almond mixture in 2 additions, beating well after each addition, until combined. Press evenly into bottom of an ungreased 9 inch (23 cm) springform pan. Bake in 350°F (175°C) oven for about 20 minutes until golden.

Beat next 3 ingredients in a large bowl until smooth. Add eggs, 1 at a time, beating after each addition until just combined.

Add next 3 ingredients and beat until just combined. Pour over crust. Bake in 325°F (160°C) oven for about 50 minutes until centre is almost set but still wobbles slightly. Immediately run a knife around inside edge of pan to allow cheesecake to settle evenly. Let stand in pan on a wire rack until cooled completely. Chill, covered, for at least 6 hours or overnight.

Spread jam evenly over cheesecake, leaving a 1/4 inch (6 mm) border. Sprinkle almonds in a lattice pattern over jam. Cuts into 12 wedges.

Black and White Cheesecake

This classy white chocolate cheesecake is nothing short of perfection. For best results, wet your knife under running warm water and wipe it clean between slices.

All-purpose flour	3/4 cup	175 mL
Cocoa, sifted if lumpy	1/4 cup	60 mL
Salt	1/8 tsp.	0.5 mL
Large eggs	2	2
Granulated sugar	1 cup	250 mL
Butter (or hard margarine), melted	1/2 cup	125 mL
Envelope of unflavoured gelatin (1/4 oz., 7 g)	1	1
Cold water	1/4 cup	60 mL
White chocolate chips	1 cup	250 mL
Block of cream cheese (8 oz., 250 g), cut up and softened	1	1
Granulated sugar	1/2 cup	125 mL
Whipping cream	3/4 cup	175 mL
Whipping cream	1/4 cup	60 mL
Dark chocolate, chopped	3 1/2 oz.	100 g

Combine first 3 ingredients in a small bowl.

Beat next 3 ingredients in a medium bowl. Add flour mixture and stir until just moistened. Spread evenly in a greased 9 inch (23 cm) springform pan. Bake in 350°F (175°C) oven for about 18 minutes until a wooden pick inserted in centre comes out moist but not wet with batter. Do not overbake. Let stand in pan on a wire rack until cooled completely.

Sprinkle gelatin over water in a small saucepan and let stand for 1 minute. Heat, stirring, on medium-low until gelatin is dissolved.

Microwave chocolate chips on medium (50%) for about 2 minutes, stirring every 30 seconds, until almost melted (see Tip, page 140). Do not overheat. Stir until smooth.

Beat cream cheese and remaining sugar in a medium bowl until combined. Add melted chocolate and gelatin mixture. Beat until smooth.

Beat first amount of whipping cream in a small bowl until soft peaks form. Fold into cream cheese mixture. Spread evenly over brownie base in pan. Chill, covered, for about 2 hours until set.

Heat second amount of whipping cream in a small saucepan on medium until hot, but not boiling. Remove from heat. Add dark chocolate and stir until smooth. Let stand for 5 minutes. Spread evenly over cheesecake. Chill for about 30 minutes until firm. Cuts into 12 wedges.

Orange, Yogurt and Poppy Seed Cheesecake

Oranges and poppy seeds are commonly used in many European cakes. We've combined these traditional partners with yogurt for a unique spin on the classic cheesecake.

Butter (or hard margarine)	1/2 cup	125 mL
Graham cracker crumbs	2 cups	500 mL
Envelopes of unflavoured gelatin (1/4 oz., 7 g, each)	2	2
Cold water	1/3 cup	75 mL
Blocks of cream cheese, (8 oz., 250 g, each), softened	2	2
Plain yogurt	1 cup	250 mL
Granulated sugar	3/4 cup	175 mL
Orange juice	1/4 cup	60 mL
Grated orange zest (see Tip, page 116)	2 tbsp.	30 mL
Poppy seeds	3 tbsp.	45 mL
Orange juice	3/4 cup	175 mL
Cornstarch	1 1/2 tbsp.	22 mL
Granulated sugar	1 tbsp.	15 mL
Orange liqueur (optional)	1 tbsp.	15 mL

Orange slices, for garnish

For the crust, melt butter in a medium saucepan on medium heat. Remove from heat and stir in graham crumbs. Press firmly in bottom and halfway up sides of an ungreased 9 inch (23 cm) springform pan. Chill for 1 hour.

For the filling, sprinkle gelatin over cold water in a small saucepan. Let stand for 1 minute. Heat, stirring, on low until gelatin is dissolved. Set aside to cool.

Beat next 5 ingredients in a large bowl until smooth. Stir in poppy seeds and gelatin mixture. Spread evenly over crust. Chill, covered, for about 3 hours until set.

For the topping, combine next 3 ingredients in a medium saucepan. Heat, stirring, on medium-high until boiling and thickened. Remove from heat. Stir in liqueur. Let stand for 1 minute. Gently spread over filling. Chill until topping is set.

Garnish with orange slices. Cuts into 12 wedges.

Mango Swirl Cheesecake

This cheesecake freezes well. It's important to completely cool it before wrapping it twice in plastic wrap, and then in foil. Freeze for up to a month, and thaw overnight in the fridge.

Butter (or hard margarine)	2/3 cup	150 mL
Graham cracker crumbs	1 3/4 cups	425 mL
Shredded coconut	2/3 cup	150 mL
Envelope of unflavoured gelatin (1/4 oz., 7 g)	1	1
Cold water	2 tbsp.	30 mL
Block of cream cheese (8 oz., 250 g), softened	1	1
Coconut milk (or reconstituted from powder)	1 cup	250 mL
Granulated sugar	1/2 cup	125 mL
Envelope of unflavoured gelatin (1/4 oz., 7 g)	1	1
Cold water	2 tbsp.	30 mL
Block of cream cheese (8 oz., 250 g), softened	1	1
Can of sliced mango in syrup (14 oz.,398 mL), drained and puréed	1	1
Granulated sugar	1/2 cup	125 mL
Drops of yellow liquid food colouring	2	2
Drop of red liquid food colouring	1	1

For the crust, melt butter in a medium saucepan on medium heat. Remove from heat. Stir in graham crumbs and coconut. Press firmly in bottom and 1 inch (2.5 cm) up side of a lightly greased 9 inch (23 cm) springform pan. Chill for 1 hour.

For the coconut filling, sprinkle gelatin over cold water in a small saucepan. Let stand for 1 minute. Heat, stirring, on low until gelatin is dissolved. Set aside to cool.

Beat next 3 ingredients in a large bowl until smooth. Beat in gelatin mixture.

For the mango filling, sprinkle gelatin over cold water in a small saucepan. Let stand for 1 minute. Heat, stirring, on low until gelatin is dissolved. Set aside to cool.

Beat next 3 ingredients in a large bowl until smooth. Beat in gelatin mixture and yellow and red food colouring. Drop spoonfuls of each filling irregularly into crust. Swirl knife through fillings to create a marble effect. Chill, covered, for at least 6 hours or overnight. Cuts into 12 wedges.

Caramel Apple Cheesecake

An apple filling is nestled in a pecan crust and topped with an elegant caramel sauce. Not your average cheesecake!

Butter	2/3 cup	150 mL
Vanilla wafer crumbs	2 cups	500 mL
Pecans, toasted (see Tip, page 148) and finely ground	1 cup	250 mL
Butter	1 tbsp.	15 mL
Cooking oil	1 tbsp.	15 mL
Chopped, peeled tart apple	3 cups	750 mL
Brown sugar, packed	1/4 cup	60 mL
Unflavoured gelatin	4 tsp.	20 mL
Apple juice	1/3 cup	75 mL
Blocks of cream cheese (8 oz., 250 g, each), softened	2	2
Sour cream	1 cup	250 mL
Granulated sugar	2/3 cup	150 mL
Ground cinnamon	1/2 tsp.	2 mL
Whipping cream	1 cup	250 mL
Pecan halves, toasted (see Tip, page 148)	24	24
MARSHMALLOW CARAMEL SAUCE		
Brown sugar, packed	2 tbsp.	30 mL
Butter	2 tbsp.	30 mL
Whipping cream	2 tbsp.	30 mL
Large white marshmallows, quartered	4	4

For the crust, melt butter in a large saucepan on medium heat. Remove from heat and stir in wafer crumbs and pecans. Press firmly in bottom and 2/3 up side of an ungreased 9 inch (23 cm) springform pan. Chill for 1 hour.

For the filling, heat next 2 ingredients in a large frying pan on medium. Add apple and cook for about 10 minutes, stirring occasionally, until apple is softened. Add brown sugar and cook, stirring, until brown sugar is dissolved. Reduce heat to low. Simmer for about 5 minutes, stirring occasionally, until thickened. Transfer to a medium bowl. Set aside to cool completely.

Sprinkle gelatin over apple juice in a small saucepan. Let stand for 1 minute. Heat, stirring, on low until gelatin is dissolved. Set aside to cool.

Beat next 4 ingredients in a large bowl until smooth. Beat in gelatin mixture. Stir in apple mixture.

Beat whipping cream in a medium bowl until soft peaks form. Fold into cream cheese mixture and spread evenly in crust. Arrange pecan halves around outside edge of cheesecake. Chill, covered, for at least 6 hours or overnight.

For the sauce, combine remaining 4 ingredients in a medium saucepan. Heat, stirring, on medium until marshmallow is melted and brown sugar is dissolved. Set aside to cool. Pour onto centre of cheesecake. Spread sauce just to edge of pecans. Chill for at least 1 hour until sauce is completely set. Cuts into 12 wedges.

Mocha-dipped Cake Pops

The only thing that separates cake balls from cake pops is the lollypop stick. To make cake balls, forego the sticks and simply set your balls on a baking pan lined with parchment paper to set. For cake pops, push the opposite end of the stick into a block of craft foam so that the cake pop stands upright as the chocolate sets.

All-purpose flour	2 cups	500 mL
Baking powder	2 tsp.	10 mL
Salt	1/2 tsp.	2 mL
Granulated sugar	1 cup	250 mL
Butter (or hard margarine), softened	1/2 cup	125 mL
Eggs	2	2
Vanilla extract	1 tsp.	5 mL
Milk	1 cup	250 mL
BUTTER ICING		
Icing (confectioner's) sugar	1 cup	250 mL
Butter	2 tbsp.	30 mL
Milk	1 1/2 tbsp.	22 mL
Vanilla extract	1/2 tsp.	5 mL
MOCHA DIP		
Semi-sweet baking chocolate, chopped	16 oz.	454 g
Strong prepared coffee or espresso	1/4 cup	60 mL
Medium unsweetened coconut	1 cup	250 mL

Combine first 8 ingredients in a medium mixing bowl. Beat slowly to moisten, then beat at medium speed until smooth, about 2 minutes. Pour into a greased 9 x 9 inch (23 x 23 cm) pan. Bake in 350°F (175°C) for 30 to 35 minutes until a wooden pick inserted in centre comes out clean. Let stand in pan on a wire rack for 10 minutes. Remove cake from pan and place on a wire rack to cool completely. Crumble cooled cake into a large bowl.

For the icing, combine next 4 ingredients in a mixing bowl and beat until smooth. Add enough icing to crumbled cake to make a mixture that is moist and holds its shape when rolled, about 1/2 cup (125 mL). Do not add too much icing or cake pops will have a soggy texture. Roll mixture into balls and place on a baking sheet. Freeze for at least 15 minutes, until firm.

Microwave 3/4 chocolate in a deep, narrow microwave-safe bowl on medium (50%) for about 2 minutes, stirring every 30 seconds, until almost melted (see Tip, page 140). Bowl should be deep enough to totally submerge cake pop. Stir in remaining 1/4 chocolate and coffee.

Microwave for about 30 seconds, until almost melted. Stir until smooth. Dip 1 end of a lollipop stick into chocolate and carefully insert into 1 cake pop, pushing no more than 1/2 way into pop. Dip pop into chocolate, ensuring entire pop is well coated and allowing any excess chocolate to drip off. Roll in coconut. Push stick into foam block so it stands upright. Repeat with remaining sticks and pops. Set aside until chocolate fully sets. Makes about 28 cake pops.

Death by Chocolate Cake Bites

Cake bites are small pieces of cake that have been dipped in chocolate. We've used a circle cookie cutter in this recipe, but you can use any shape you prefer. Leftover bits of cake can be crumbled and made into cake pops (see page 134). You can also skip the cookie cutter altogether and simply cut your cake into small squares. Refrigerate these bites to make then set faster, if you prefer. Otherwise they need a few hours to set, so plan accordingly. Any dense cake works well for cake bites. We've chosen the brownie-like Mississippi Mud Cake, but a pound cake would also work beautifully.

Mississippi Mud Cake, page 52 (cake only, no topping or icing), partially frozen (see Tip, below)	1	1
Semi-sweet baking chocolate, chopped	16 oz.	454 g
Butter (not margarine)	1/4 cup	60 mL

Cut shapes out of cake with a small round cookie cutter. Place cake circles on a baking pan lined with parchment paper.

Microwave 3/4 chocolate and butter in a deep, narrow microwave-safe bowl on medium (50%) for about 2 minutes, stirring every 30 seconds, until almost melted (see Tip, page 140). Bowl should be deep enough to totally submerge cake bite. Stir in remaining 1/4 chocolate. Microwave for about 30 seconds, until almost melted. Stir until smooth. Dip cake shapes in chocolate, 1 at a time, ensuring entire bite is well coated and allowing any excess chocolate to drip off. Place on baking pan (see **Note**). Set aside until chocolate fully sets. Before serving, for a cleaner look, you can trim bottoms of pooled chocolate, if you prefer. Makes 18 small circle bites.

Note: Instead of dipping the bites, you can also pour the chocolate overtop, if you prefer. With this method, the bottom surface of the cake will not be coated with chocolate.

Tip: Partially freezing the cake makes it easier to cut without crumbling, which will also make it easier to dip.

Cone Cupcakes

A fun and unexpected way to serve any cupcake variety. We've gone with white cupcakes topped with a light peanut butter icing, but the possibilities are endless!

Butter (or hard margarine)	1/2 cup	125 mL
Granulated sugar	1 cup	250 mL
Large eggs	2	2
Vanilla extract	1 tsp.	5 mL
All-purpose flour	1 3/4 cup	425 mL
Baking powder	2 1/2 tsp.	12 mL
Salt	1/4 tsp.	1 mL
Milk	2/3 cup	150 mL
Flat-bottomed ice cream cones	24	24

Peanut Butter Icing, page 86

Beat butter and sugar together in a medium bowl. Add eggs 1 at a time, beating well after each addition. Stir in vanilla.

Combine next 3 ingredients in a small bowl.

Add flour mixture and milk alternately to butter mixture, beginning and ending with flour. Fill cones about 3/4 full, leaving batter 1/2 inch (12 mm) from top. Place filled cones on baking sheet. Bake in 375°F (190°C) oven for 15 to 20 minutes until a wooden pick inserted in centre comes out clean. Let stand until cool.

Ice tops of cupcakes with Peanut Butter Icing. Makes 24 cupcake cones.

Chocolate Molten Cakes

You don't have to go to a fancy restaurant to enjoy a molten lava cake anymore. This recipe makes it easy to recreate this fantastic wonder at home. What's the trick? Just don't overbake it!

Cocoa, sifted if lumpy	1 tbsp.	15 mL
Butter (or hard margarine)	2/3 cup	150 mL
Dark chocolate, chopped	3 1/2 oz.	100 g
Large eggs	4	4
Granulated sugar	1 cup	250 mL
All-purpose flour	1/2 cup	125 mL
Cocoa, sifted if lumpy	1/4 cup	60 mL

Coat bottom and sides of 8 greased 3/4 cup (175 mL) ramekins with first amount of cocoa. Discard any remaining cocoa. Place on a baking sheet with sides.

Heat butter and chocolate in a small saucepan on lowest heat, stirring often, until almost melted (see Tip, below). Remove from heat. Stir until smooth. Set aside to cool slightly.

Beat eggs and sugar in a medium bowl for about 5 minutes until thick and pale.

Add flour, second amount of cocoa and butter mixture. Beat until smooth. Pour into prepared ramekins (see **Note**). Bake in 400°F (200°C) oven for about 10 minutes until edges and top are set but wooden pick inserted in centre is still wet with batter. Let stand for 5 minutes. Makes 8 cakes.

Note: Ramekins can be covered and chilled at this point for up to 1 day. Bake from chilled for about 11 minutes until edges and top are set but wooden pick inserted in centre is wet with batter.

Tip: Always melt chocolate over low heat. A high temperature will scorch chocolate, creating a grainy texture. Chocolate continues melting after it's removed from heat, so finish melting it away from the heat, stirring until it's smooth and glossy. Never cover melting chocolate. This causes condensation, and even the tiniest drop of water will cause the chocolate to seize and become lumpy.

Chocolate Jelly Roll

For a simple look, dust the roll with icing sugar. If you are feeling a little fancier, dress it up by icing it with whipped cream.

Large eggs	4	4
Granulated sugar	2/3 cup	150 mL
Vanilla extract	1/2 tsp.	2 mL
All-purpose flour	3/4 cup	175 mL
Cocoa, sifted	1/3 cup	75 mL
Warm water	4 tsp.	20 mL
Icing (confectioner's) sugar, for dusting		
CHOCOLATE BUTTER ICING		
Butter (not margarine), softened	3/4 cup	175 mL
Boiling water	1/4 cup	60 mL
Vanilla	1/2 tsp.	2 mL
Icing (confectioner's) sugar	2 cups	500 mL
Cocoa, sifted if lumpy	1/4 cup	60 mL

Combine eggs, sugar and vanilla in a medium bowl. Beat well until thick enough to leave a trail when beaters are lifted. Should be thick and mousse-like.

Sift flour and cocoa onto a plate. Fold into batter. Add water and fold together. Spread evenly in a greased 10 x 15 inch (25 x 38 cm) jelly roll pan lined with waxed paper. Bake in 400°F (200°C) oven for 10 to 12 minutes until a wooden pick inserted in centre comes out clean. Turn out onto a tea towel dusted with icing sugar. Remove waxed paper, and trim crisp edges off cake. Roll up from short end in a clean tea towel and set aside to cool.

For the filling, beat remaining 5 ingredients in a medium bowl until mixture lightens in both colour and texture. Unroll cake when cool and spread icing to edges. Roll up without towel. Cuts into 12 slices.

Chocolate Charlotte Russe

Ladyfingers form the base and sides of this smooth, unique cake. For an added chocolate touch, one end of each ladyfinger is dipped in melted chocolate.

Envelopes of unflavoured gelatin (1/4 oz., 7 g, each)	2	2
Milk	2 1/2 cups	625 mL
Granulated sugar	2/3 cup	150 mL
Cocoa, sifted if lumpy	1/2 cup	125 mL
Salt	1/4 tsp.	1 mL
Egg yolks (large)	3	3
Milk	2 tbsp.	30 mL
Vanilla extract	1 tsp.	5 mL
Egg whites (large), room temperature (see Tip, page 146)	3	3
Granulated sugar	1/3 cup	75 mL
Frozen whipped topping, thawed (or 1 envelope of dessert topping, prepared)	2 cups	500 mL
Giant ladyfingers	30	30
Semi-sweet baking chocolate, melted (see Tip, page 140)	8 oz.	225 g

Sprinkle gelatin over first amount of milk in a medium saucepan. Let stand for 1 minute. Heat, stirring, on low until gelatin is dissolved. Bring to a boil.

Combine next 3 ingredients in a small bowl.

Stir in next 3 ingredients. Add to boiling gelatin mixture, stirring constantly, until just thickened. Set saucepan in a bowl of ice water. Let stand, stirring and scraping down sides often, until mixture will mound slightly. The mixture will thicken quickly as it cools.

Beat egg whites in a medium bowl until soft peaks form. Add second amount of sugar, 1 tbsp. (15 mL) at a time, beating constantly until stiff peaks form and sugar is dissolved. Fold into gelatin mixture.

Fold in whipped topping.

Cut 1 inch (2.5 cm) piece off 1 end of each ladyfinger. Set pieces aside. Dip one end of each ladyfinger in chocolate, alternating between round end and cut end. Stand ladyfingers rounded-side out, cut-side down around inside edge of a greased 10 inch (25 cm) springform pan.

Lay remaining ladyfingers and reserved pieces in a single layer in bottom of pan, breaking to fit as necessary. Spoon gelatin mixture into pan, keeping ladyfingers upright. Chill until firm. Cuts into 10 wedges.

Gooey Cookie Crumble Cake

This delicious treat will have even the most refined person greedily licking their plate clean. The rich combination of cookies, cream cheese, peanut butter, pecans and chocolate is irresistible.

Butter (or hard margarine)	1/4 cup	60 mL
Smooth peanut butter	3 tbsp.	45 mL
Oreo cookie crumbs	1 1/2 cups	375 mL
Finely chopped pecans	1/2 cup	125 mL
Block of cream cheese (8 oz., 250 g), softened	1	1
Granulated sugar	1/2 cup	125 mL
Smooth peanut butter	1/2 cup	125 mL
Large eggs (see Tip, below)	2	2
Milk	2 tbsp.	30 mL
Vanilla extract	1 1/2 tsp.	7 mL
Frozen whipped topping, thawed (or whipped cream)	4 cups	1 L
Butterscotch ice cream topping	1/4 cup	60 mL
Chocolate ice cream topping	1/4 cup	60 mL

For the crust, melt butter in a medium saucepan on medium heat. Remove from heat and stir in peanut butter until smooth. Add cookie crumbs and pecans. Stir well. Reserve 1/2 cup (125 mL) for topping. Press remaining mixture firmly in an ungreased 9 x 13 inch (23 x 33 cm) pan.

For the filling, beat next 3 ingredients in a large bowl until smooth. Add eggs, 1 at a time, beating well after each addition. Add milk and vanilla. Mix well.

Fold in whipped topping. Spread evenly over crust.

For the topping, drizzle butterscotch and chocolate ice cream toppings over filling. Sprinkle with reserved crumb mixture. Freeze, covered, for at least 6 hours or overnight. Let stand at room temperature for about 10 minutes before cutting. Cuts into 15 pieces.

Tip: When preparing recipes that use raw egg, make sure to use fresh, uncracked, clean Grade A eggs. Pregnant women, young children and the elderly are not advised to eat anything containing raw egg.

Chilly Banana Split Cake

Each layered wedge packs in all the delicious flavours of a banana split.

Graham cracker crumbs	1 1/4 cups	300 mL
Butter (or hard margarine), melted	1/2 cup	125 mL
Medium sweetened coconut	1/3 cup	75 mL
Sliced banana	1 1/2 cups	375 mL
Vanilla ice cream, softened	4 cups	1 L
Sliced fresh strawberries	1 cup	250 mL
Can of crushed pineapple (14 oz., 398 mL), drained	1	1
Chopped maraschino cherries	1/4 cup	60 mL
Medium sweetened coconut, toasted (see Tip, below)	2 tbsp.	30 mL
Chocolate ice cream topping	3/4 cup	175 mL

Combine first 3 ingredients in a small bowl. Press firmly into bottom and 1/2 inch (12 mm) up sides of ungreased 9 inch (23 cm) springform pan.

Arrange banana slices over crumb mixture.

Spread half of ice cream evenly over banana. Arrange strawberries over ice cream. Spread remaining ice cream evenly over strawberries. Scatter pineapple and cherries over top. Sprinkle with coconut. Cover with plastic wrap. Freeze for at least 6 hours or overnight. Let stand at room temperature for about 20 minutes to soften slightly before serving.

Drizzle ice cream topping over entire cake or individual servings. Cuts into 12 wedges.

Tip: When toasting nuts, seeds or coconut, cooking times will vary for each ingredient, so never toast them together. For small amounts, cook the ingredient in an ungreased frying pan on medium for 3 to 5 minutes, stirring often. For larger amounts, spread the ingredient evenly in an ungreased shallow pan and bake in a 350°F (175°C) oven for 5 to 10 minutes, stirring or shaking often, until golden.

Chocolate Layered Cake

Amaretti is the Italian name for macaroons. Crisp and crunchy on the outside and soft on the inside, these cookies, and their crumbs, are perfect for absorbing the orange liqueur. If your grocer doesn't carry them, try an Italian food store.

Package of amaretti cookies (7 oz., 200 g)	1	1
Orange liqueur	1/4 cup	60 mL
Dark chocolate bars (3 1/2 oz., 100 g, each), chopped	5	5
Butter (or hard margarine)	1/2 cup	125 mL
Egg yolks (large)	2	2
Whipping cream	1 cup	250 mL
Sliced fresh strawberries	3 cups	750 mL
Icing (confectioner's) sugar	1/4 cup	60 mL

Line bottom and sides of a greased 9 inch (23 cm) springform pan with parchment (not waxed) paper. Process cookies in a blender or food processor to form coarse crumbs. Transfer to a medium bowl. Stir in liqueur. Let stand for 10 minutes.

Combine chocolate and butter in a medium heavy saucepan on lowest heat, stirring often, until chocolate is almost melted (see Tip, page 140). Do not overheat. Remove from heat and stir until smooth.

Add egg yolks, 1 at a time, stirring well after each addition. Set aside to cool.

Beat whipping cream in a small bowl until soft peaks form. Fold into chocolate mixture. Spread 1/3 of whipped cream mixture in prepared pan. Carefully sprinkle with half of cookie mixture, patting crumbs down lightly. Spread with half of remaining whipped cream mixture. Sprinkle with remaining cookie mixture. Pat crumbs down lightly. Carefully spread remaining whipped cream mixture evenly over top. Chill, covered, for at least 6 hours or overnight until set.

Arrange strawberries on top. Sprinkle with icing sugar. Cuts into 10 wedges.

White Chocolate Orange Chill

White chocolate and orange—how could anyone resist this tantalizing combination?

Butter (or hard margarine)	1/3 cup	75 mL
Oreo cookie crumbs	1 1/2 cups	375 mL
Granulated sugar	1/2 cup	125 mL
Orange juice	1/2 cup	125 mL
Frozen concentrated orange juice	1/4 cup	60 mL
Orange liqueur (or orange juice)	1/4 cup	60 mL
Lemon juice	1 tsp.	5 mL
Salt	1/8 tsp.	0.5 mL
Envelope of unflavoured gelatin (1/4 oz., 7 g)	1	1
Cold water	1/4 cup	60 mL
Whipped topping	2 cups	500 mL
Grated white chocolate	1/2 cup	125 mL

White chocolate curls, for garnish
Orange slices, for garnish
Whipped cream, for garnish
Chocolate chips, for garnish

For the crust, melt butter in a medium saucepan on medium heat. Remove from heat and stir in cookie crumbs. Press firmly in bottom and 1 inch (2.5 cm) up sides of an ungreased 8 inch (20 cm) springform pan. Set aside to chill.

For the filling, combine next 6 ingredients in a large bowl.

Sprinkle gelatin over cold water in a small saucepan. Let stand for 1 minute. Heat, stirring, on low until gelatin is dissolved. Add to orange juice mixture, stirring until sugar is dissolved. Set aside to cool slightly.

Fold in whipped topping until no white streaks remain.

Gently fold in chocolate. Spread evenly in crust. Freeze until set.

Garnish with chocolate curls, orange slices, whipped cream and chocolate chips. Cuts into 12 wedges.

Frozen Mocha Cheesecake

This awesome, rich dessert is the perfect fix for those times when your sweet tooth just won't be denied. Simply cut off a slice or two and put the rest back into the freezer—a treat in no time.

Butter (or hard margarine)	1/2 cup	125 mL
Graham cracker crumbs	1 1/2 cups	375 mL
Granulated sugar	1/4 cup	60 mL
Cocoa, sifted if lumpy	1/4 cup	60 mL
Block of cream cheese (8 oz., 250 g), softened	1	1
Can of sweetened condensed milk (11 oz., 300 mL)	1	1
Chocolate ice cream topping	2/3 cup	150 mL
Instant coffee granules	1 tbsp.	15 mL
Hot water	1 tsp.	5 mL
Whipping cream (or 1 envelope of dessert topping, prepared)	1 cup	250 mL

For the crust, melt butter in a medium saucepan on medium heat. Remove from heat and stir in next 3 ingredients. Reserve 1/2 cup (125 mL) for topping. Press remaining mixture firmly in bottom and 1 inch (2.5 cm) up sides of ungreased 9 inch (23 cm) springform pan.

For the filling, beat cream cheese in a medium bowl until smooth. Add condensed milk and ice cream topping. Mix well.

Dissolve coffee granules in hot water. Stir into cream cheese mixture.

Beat whipping cream in a medium bowl until soft peaks form. Fold into cream cheese mixture. Spread evenly in crust. Sprinkle with reserved crumb mixture. Freeze until firm. Cuts into 8 wedges.

Tres Leches Cake

White cake saturated with a mixture of three forms of milk and rum. Looks plain but tastes deliciously complex. The cake must chill overnight, so plan accordingly.

All-purpose flour	2 cups	500 mL
Baking powder	2 tsp.	10 mL
Baking soda	1/2 tsp.	2 mL
Salt	1/4 tsp.	1 mL
Butter (or hard margarine), softened	1/2 cup	125 mL
Granulated sugar	1 cup	250 mL
Large eggs	2	2
Vanilla extract	1 tsp.	5 mL
Buttermilk	1 1/2 cups	375 mL
Can of evaporated milk (13 oz., 370 mL)	1	1
Can of sweetened condensed milk (11 oz., 300 mL)	1	1
Milk	1/2 cup	125 mL
Light rum	1/3 cup	75 mL
Whipping cream	1 cup	250 mL
Instant vanilla pudding powder	1 tbsp.	15 mL

Combine first 4 ingredients in a medium bowl.

Beat butter and sugar in a large bowl until light and fluffy. Add eggs, 1 at a time, beating well after each addition. Beat in vanilla.

Add flour mixture in 3 additions, alternating with buttermilk in 2 additions, stirring after each addition until just combined. Spread evenly in a greased, foil-lined 9 x 13 inch (23 x 33 cm) pan. Bake in 350°F (175°C) oven for 25 to 30 minutes until a wooden pick inserted in centre of cake comes out clean. Place on a wire rack. Using a wooden skewer, poke random holes into cake.

Stir next 4 ingredients in a medium bowl. Slowly spoon over warm cake, allowing cake to absorb milk mixture before adding more. Chill, covered, overnight.

Beat whipping cream and pudding powder in a medium bowl until stiff peaks form. Spread onto cake. Cuts into 16 pieces.

Index